The Changing Fortunes of Economic Liberalism: Yesterday, Today and Tomorrow

David Henderson

With an Introduction by Nigel Lawson

and

a Text by Milton Friedman

Published by the Institute of Economic Affairs, 1998

First published in November 1998 by
The Institute of Economic Affairs
2 Lord North Street
Westminster
London SW1P 3LB

Occasional Paper 105
ISSN 0073-909X
ISBN 0-255 36419-9

Printed in Great Britain by
Hartington Fine Arts Limited, Lancing, West Sussex
Set in Times Roman 11 on 13 point

Contents

Editor's Note   *Professor Colin Robinson*   5

A Text from Milton Friedman   7

Introduction   *Lord Lawson of Blaby*   11

Author's Preface   15

The Author   16

Part 1: Theme and Setting   17

A Framework for the Story   17

Character of the Hero   19

Background and Point of Departure   26

Part 2: The Uneasy Trend to Economic Liberalism   34

A General View Across the World   34

Groups of Countries and Areas of Policy   42

The Evolving International Economic System: 'Globalisation' and its Effects   58

Summing Up: Developments over Twenty Years   65

Part 3: Interpreting the Trend   68

The Political Dimension   68

Interests, Ideas and Liberal Gains   71

Liberalism's Chronic Weakness   81

Accounting for Liberalisation   90

Part 4: Will the Trend to Economic Liberalism Continue?   98

Consolidation, Momentum and Spread   98

The Impact and Lessons of Recent Crises   100

3

Old Limits and New Threats	104
Part 5: Epilogue: A 120-Year Perspective	111
A Century-long Retreat	112
Has the Climate of Opinion Really Changed?	117
An Achievement and Its Limits	120
Annex: Measuring Economic Freedom and Assessing Its Benefits	123

Table 1: 1975-1995: The Geography of Economic Reform	35
Table 2: Combined Economic Freedom Ratings, 1975-95	38
Table 3: Changes in Economic Freedom Ratings for 54 Reforming Countries, 1975-95	40-41
Table 4: Public Expenditure Ratios, 1970-96, for 13 Core OECD Countries, Selected Years	52
Table 5: Growth Rates of World Output and Exports, 1820-1997	60

Summary	*Back cover*

Editor's Note

AS DAVID HENDERSON explains in his author's preface, this paper began life as a talk given at the October 1997 Economic Freedom of the World Conference in Britain. In the talk, David took as a starting point a reported summary assessment of the long-term evolution of economic freedom of the United States which had been made by Milton Friedman, who has been one of the moving spirits in the Economic Freedom of the World project and also a consistent supporter of the IEA from its early years. In preparing the present paper the same approach has been taken – there is a text, which again is taken from Milton Friedman. This time, however, the text is not a reported statement but the summing-up of long-term historical trends in the United States by Friedman and his wife Rose Friedman in their recently published memoirs. The relevant extract from the memoirs is reprinted here (pp. 7-9) with the authors' and publisher's permission.

Following Professor Friedman's Text is an Introduction by Lord Lawson of Blaby, who held several senior Cabinet positions (including Chancellor of the Exchequer) during the 1980s, who carefully places David Henderson's paper in the context of recent world economic developments.

David Henderson's paper follows the Introduction. As with all IEA papers it represents the views of the author, not those of the Institute (which has no corporate view), its Trustees, Advisers or Directors. It is published at a time when governments' commitments to liberal market ideas are under test. The intention is to stimulate discussion on the important issues which Henderson identifies.

October 1998   COLIN ROBINSON
Editorial Director, Institute of Economic Affairs;
Professor of Economics, University of Surrey

A Text
from MILTON FRIEDMAN

WHEN JOHN BLUNDELL ASKED ME if I would care to write a response to the article by David Henderson, I recalled that Rose and I had written a statement about essentially the same subject as the Epilogue of our forthcoming book, *Two Lucky People: Memoirs*, published by the University of Chicago Press in 1998.[1] What follows is a relevant excerpt from that Epilogue.

Milton Friedman

'The world at the end of our life is very different from the world in which we grew up, in some ways enormously better, in other ways, worse. Materially, the wonders of science and enterprise have enormously enriched the world though some products of science, like atomic energy, have been a mixed blessing. Few monarchs of ancient times could have lived as well as we have. In the course of our own lifetime, we have been treated to automatic washing machines, dryers and dishwashers; microwaves; radio, television, computers, cellular phones; passenger airlines, first prop, then jet; and so on and on.

'Biologically, advances in medicine have lengthened life spans. Milton has lived decades longer than his father thanks to such advances. Life expectancy in the United States is almost 50 per cent higher now than when we were born. Equally important, medical advances have lessened pain and suffering, and improved the quality of life at all ages.

'The situation is far less clear-cut in the social realm. Perhaps it is simply nostalgia, but we recall our youth as a period when there was far less concern for personal safety and safety of property. It was not unusual to leave home without locking doors; people worried less about walking about at night. One indication that this is more than nostalgia is that the fraction of the population in prison

---

[1] Milton and Rose D. Friedman, *Two Lucky People*: *Memoirs*, Chicago: University of Chicago Press, 1998.

today is three times as large as it was in 1928 – though that was the period of prohibition of alcohol and the notorious Capone gangsters.

'Physicians and hospitals did not have the amazing array of medications, tests, techniques, and equipment that they have now, but there is little doubt that there was a healthier relation among patient, physician, and hospital. The first question a patient faced was not, 'What insurance do you have?' but 'What is wrong?'.

'The income tax did not apply to most people, and was a page or two in length for those who had to file. Governments at all levels were controlling the spending of 10 to 15 per cent of the national income.

'In one sense, we are freer now than then – there is far more tolerance for unconventional behaviour (though recall that the twenties were the era of the flapper), less anti-Semitism and less prejudice against blacks and Catholics. In another sense, we are less free. We are close to being enmeshed in that "network of petty, complicated rules that are both minute and uniform" that de Tocqueville conjectured might be the inevitable effect of an excessive drive to equality.[2] There doubtless are many causes for the loss of freedom, but surely a major cause has been the growth of government and its increasing control of our lives. Today, government, directly or indirectly, controls the spending of as much as half of our national income.

'Our central theme in public advocacy has been the promotion of human freedom. That was encouraged by our participation in the Mont Pelerin and Philadelphia Societies. It is the theme of our books, *Capitalism and Freedom* and *Free to Choose;* it underlies our opposition to rent control and general wage and price controls, our support for educational choice, privatising radio and television channels, an all-volunteer army, limitation of government spending, legalisation of drugs, privatising social security, free trade, and the deregulation of industry and private life to the fullest extent possible.

'Judged by practice, we have, despite some successes, mostly been on the losing side. Judged by ideas, we have been on the

---

[2] Alexis de Tocqueville, *Democracy in America,* Anchor Books edition, Garden City, N.Y.: Doubleday & Company, Inc., 1969, p.692.

winning side. The public in the United States has increasingly recognised that government is not the universal cure for all ills, that governmental measures taken with good intentions and for good purposes often, if not typically, go astray and do harm instead of good. The growth of government has come to a halt, and seems on the verge of declining as a fraction of the economy. We are in the mainstream of thought, not as we were 50 years ago, members of the derided minority.

'So we close this book full of optimism for the future. Our children and grandchildren will live in a country that continues to advance rapidly in material and biological well-being, and that gives its citizens ever wider freedom to follow their own values and tastes, so long as they do not interfere with the ability of others to do the same.'

October 1998   MILTON AND ROSE D. FRIEDMAN

Introduction
by LORD LAWSON OF BLABY

LIKE MANY OTHERS, I first came across David Henderson, rather belatedly, when he delivered his outstanding 1985 series of Reith Lectures, *Innocence and Design: the influence of economic ideas on policy.* Yet despite that *tour de force* he has remained singularly little known outside his own profession. This may well be because his style, while admirably lucid, is unusually fair-minded, moderate, respectful of the facts, and averse to polemic – qualities that are well displayed in this new book, whose publication turns out to be rather more appositely timed than he can have imagined when he started to write it.

After an excellent description of economic liberalism, Henderson carefully charts its remarkable comeback, pretty well throughout the world, over the past 20 years, and provides a measured and convincing explanation of why this has happened. But will it continue? A committed economic (and political) liberal himself, Henderson's verdict is far from the triumphalism of a Fukuyama: 'Despite their substantial improvement over these past two decades', he concludes, 'which appears all the more notable when seen in historical perspective, the fortunes of economic liberalism during the opening decades of the new century remain clouded and in doubt.' (p. 121)

Henderson gives two principal reasons for the political fragility of economic liberalism. The first, which he characterises as its chronic weakness, is that 'economic liberalism as such has no solid basis of general support'. That is not to say that there is public support for full-blooded collectivism, either. It is rather that the general public, at all levels, continues to subscribe to what Henderson in his 1985 Reith Lectures somewhat dismissively christened 'do-it-yourself economics': a ragbag of intuitively persuasive fallacies (such as that economic competition is predominantly between states), usefully summarised in this book, all of which have a distinctly interventionist flavour.

As Henderson demonstrates with a few well-chosen quotations, DIYE is particularly well entrenched at the highest levels of the European Community; but it is prevalent everywhere. He seems to believe that this is at least partly because there is no well-supported political party in any major country which explicitly stands first and foremost for classical liberalism. I have some reservations about this. In the first place, while strictly (and unsurprisingly) true, the profound strain of scepticism, about human nature and government alike, which lies at the heart of British Conservatism, clearly provides the soil in which economic liberalism is likely to flourish, as it did during the 1980s in particular. And in the second place, I would feel more secure if economic liberalism were part of the consensus or common ground between the political parties, as it was throughout most of the last century and if 'new Labour' is to mean anything should become again, than if it were to remain the unique creed of one of them.

The second reason for fearing that the worldwide trend in favour of economic liberalism, which has been such a feature of the past 20 years, may not persist, is of course the financial and economic turmoil that has engulfed many of the emerging countries of the world and now threatens the rest.

Economic liberalism was the established orthodoxy, in both the United Kingdom and the United States, and to a considerable extent in Continental Europe too, throughout the 19th century and right up to the First World War. The result was a century and more of outstanding economic, technological, political and civic development. It was not until the apparent malfunctioning of the capitalist free market economy in the 1920s and even more the 1930s, marked in particular by unprecedented levels of unemployment, that politicians came to believe that the future lay with collectivism and large-scale government intervention in the economy.

But the cure turned out to be worse than the disease. The 20th-century experiment with big interventionist government turned out at best to be a severe disappointment, and at worst a major disaster. Hence the comeback of economic liberalism over the past 20 years.

Are we now about to see yet another swing of the pendulum? Rationally, it is hard to see why we should. The major source of weakness in the world economy today, Japan, the world's second largest economy, is in difficulty for a number of reasons, but none of them has anything to do with the unregulated nature of international capital markets (Japan has been a consistent capital exporter) or any other free market phenomena. The collapse of the much smaller and therefore much less important 'tiger' economies of East Asia is a different story; but even here, when a ship almost sinks in a heavy storm, does one seek a remedy in trying to prevent storm conditions, which are bound to arise from time to time, or in making the vessel properly seaworthy?

During the 1930s it was understandable that many people felt that capitalism was in terminal crisis. In the light of subsequent history, there are no grounds for believing this today. During the 1930s it was understandable that many felt that collectivism and interventionism might be the way ahead. Given the disaster of the collectivist and interventionist experiment that ensued, it is hard to see how anyone can rationally believe this today.

Nonetheless, if our leaders are so foolish as to allow the present difficulties to lead to a world slump, economic liberalism might indeed be snuffed out once again, to the great cost of the peoples of the world. But there is no reason why they should be so foolish. For while there is no averting a downturn, we know now how to prevent a collapse – even if the world's bankers still have a few lessons to learn in how to assess the true risks of derivatives.

At the end of the day, there are just four simple rules. *First*, the soundness of, and confidence in, the major banking systems of the world need to be maintained, should it become necessary, in the way Bagehot set out more than a century ago. *Second,* the world's leading monetary authorities need to demonstrate, as they did in the wake of black Monday in 1987, that they stand shoulder to shoulder in the face of the common threat. *Third*, they need to stand ready, again should it become necessary, to use monetary policy to prevent a decline in the money supply. And *fourth*, the governments of the world need to maintain open markets for international trade, come what may. Just stick to these four rules and, however rough the going gets, there will be no world depression.

October 1998   LORD LAWSON OF BLABY

Author's Preface

THIS ESSAY STARTED LIFE as a talk given to the Economic Freedom of the World conference held in Berlin in October 1997, and I have kept the personal flavour of the presentation then. As compared with the talk, the present text is greatly extended and enlarged. Even so, it is no more than a sketch, since it covers a leading aspect of the evolution of economic policies across the world over the past two decades.

I would like to thank John Blundell, General Director of the Institute of Economic Affairs, for suggesting that I should turn the original talk into a published essay, and Colin Robinson, the Institute's Editorial Director, for watching over the process of evolution into a document longer than either of us had anticipated.

In first revising the talk, I received discerning comments on the text from two former OECD Secretariat colleagues, Jørgen Elmeskov and Michael Klein, and help with some of the data from Neena Sapra of the IEA. At the second stage, in preparing the revised draft for publication, I benefited greatly from comments and suggestions from David Briggs, Jørgen Elmeskov, Helen Hughes, Michael Irwin, Eric Jones, Roger Kerr, Wilfrid Legg, Pierre Poret, David Robertson, Maurice Scott and Bryce Wilkinson. Finally, I revised the ordering of the text substantially in response to suggestions from both Colin Robinson and Milton Friedman. My thanks are due to all.

The work of preparing the Berlin talk was carried out in Paris, where I was attached to the Groupe d'Economie Mondiale directed by Professor Patrick Messerlin at the Fondation Nationale des Sciences Politiques. Extensive revision was undertaken while I was likewise a visitor, first at the Melbourne Business School, where Professor John Rose is Director and I was attached to the Centre for Trade Practice headed by Professor David Robertson, and later at the New Zealand Business Roundtable of which Roger Kerr is Executive Director. I am grateful to all three institutions and their respective heads for the facilities and encouragement which they kindly provided.

October 1998   DAVID HENDERSON

The Author

DAVID HENDERSON was formerly Head of the Economics and Statistics Department of the Organisation for Economic Co-operation and Development in Paris. Before that he had worked as an academic (first in Oxford University, and later at University College, London), as a British civil servant (first in HM Treasury, and later the Ministry of Aviation), and as a staff member of the World Bank. Since leaving the OECD he has been an independent author and consultant, and has served as visiting fellow or professor at institutions in Britain, France, Belgium, Australia and New Zealand. In 1985 he gave the BBC Reith Lectures which were published under the title *Innocence and Design: The Influence of Economic Ideas on Policy*. He is an Honorary Fellow of Lincoln College, Oxford, and in 1992 he was made Commander of the Order of St Michael and St George (CMG).

Part 1: Theme and Setting

OVER THE PAST TWO DECADES, economic policies across the world, and economic systems with them, have changed their character, their complexion. To an extent that few anticipated before the event, a large and growing array of governments have adopted measures, and in some cases whole programmes, with the intention and the effect of making their economies freer, more open and less regulated: both individually and in concert, they have taken the path of economic reform.

Admittedly, and not surprisingly, the picture is an untidy one. There remains a long list of countries in which no such shift in policies has occurred, including some where the trend has been the other way. In the reforming countries themselves, the process has typically been fitful, erratic, and subject to exceptions, limitations and local reverses, while the timing, scope and content of reform have varied greatly from case to case. But looking at the world as a whole over the past 20 years, the general direction of change is clear. On balance, national economic systems have become more market-oriented, and international transactions less subject to restrictions and discrimination. True, this was not solely due to the unconstrained actions of governments: official policies have interacted, in a mutually reinforcing process, with technical and economic factors which were to a large extent independent of them. But the main single influence on events has been a deliberate re-orientation of the economic policies of an increasing number of national states.

A Framework for the Story

These developments have been widely interpreted as a victory for conservatism: economic reform is seen as involving, even presupposing, a shift to the right in political terms. This, however, is a mistaken interpretation of history. Despite the early and continuing prominence in the reform process of those eminent self-proclaimed conservatives, Margaret Thatcher and Ronald Reagan, conservatism is not the central character, the unifying theme, in this particular set of episodes. As will be seen, the reforming governments of these past 20 years have come from widely separated locations on the conventional political spectrum; and in any case, now as in earlier periods, the actual reforms did not

17

embody conservative ideas or principles. The supposed connection with conservatism is a false trail.

More justly, the recent evolution of economic policies can be seen as the latest chapter in a continuing story which goes back at any rate to the mid-18th century, the hero of which is economic liberalism. Recent events have involved a shift, not from left to right, but in the balance between liberalism and interventionism in economic systems. Economic reform is a process of *liberalisation*.

How far this framework can be applied generally, to all the many countries involved, is admittedly a matter of debate. Herbert Stein, in a perceptive review of Robert Skidelsky's book, *The World after Communism*, says of Skidelsky's vision of a world-wide present-day trend away from collectivism towards greater freedom that it

> 'includes as essentially similar the fall of Communism in the Soviet Union and the emergence of Thatcherism in Britain and Reaganism in the United States. Now these developments do have some things in common, just as a beheading and a haircut have something in common. But the differences are so great that to discuss them as part of the same continuum is misleading'.[1]

I think Stein is right in two respects. The changes in the former Soviet Union and the Western democracies were largely independent of one another, while the respective points of departure were quite different. Skidelsky writes of a shift from 'collectivism' to 'liberalism' which is common to both groups of countries, but the 'collectivism' of Jimmy Carter, Valéry Giscard d'Estaing, Harold Wilson and Malcolm Fraser is not to be put on a par with that of Stalin, Brezhnev and Mao. In the West, reforms have brought with them a shift in emphasis within economies which were market-based before and after the event. In the former Soviet Union and in Central and Eastern Europe, a recasting of the whole system was and is involved.

All the same, there are similarities as well as differences. In the measures of liberalisation that have been adopted across the world, in former communist countries as elsewhere, there are obvious common features and aims. Despite the huge disparities between

---

[1] Herbert Stein, 'Out From Under', a review of Robert Skidelsky, *The World after Communism: A Polemic for Our Times*, London: Macmillan, 1995. In America the book is entitled *The Road from Serfdom*.

economic and political systems at the start of the various reform processes, and differences also in the content and timing of change, the element of liberalisation has been clearly present in both groups of countries, and in others too. In all these cases, the fortunes of economic liberalism have improved. It is not mistaken to see this as a world-wide tendency.

I present, in Part 2 below, a summary account of what I have termed 'the uneasy trend' to economic liberalism over this recent period. In doing so, I consider how far the main conclusions of Milton and Rose Friedman in relation to long-term trends in the US, as given in the Epilogue to their memoirs that is reprinted above (pp. 7-9) are applicable to the world in general over the past 20 years. The main emphasis here is on the events themselves – the content, extent and sequence of reforms. In Part 3 I consider how these events are to be explained and interpreted, with a view in particular to assessing how far economic liberalism has gained in status and influence across the world, and whether the influences that have brought the shift in policies are likely to persist. In this section, therefore, the past is treated not just for its own sake but also as a guide to the future. Part 4 is more directly focused on future possibilities, though it includes some reference to the current crises in a number of East Asian countries as well as a brief review of some longer-term and more general factors, adverse and favourable, which bear on the prospects for continuing economic reform.[2] I conclude with an epilogue which places the story of liberalisation over these past two decades in a much broader historical context, going back well over a century. The remainder of Part 1 provides a background and point of departure for the main argument.

Character of the Hero

I use the term 'liberalism' here in its European rather than its usual American sense. In standard current American usage – to which,

---

[2] All these are also the themes of the recently published book by Daniel Yergin and Joseph Stanislaw, *The Commanding Heights: The Battle between Government and the Marketplace That Is Remaking the Modern World*, New York: Simon and Schuster, 1997, which however provides a much more extended treatment including (to quote the dust-jacket) 'compelling tales of the astute politicians, brilliant thinkers, and tenacious businessmen who brought these changes about'.

however, the Friedmans do not conform – a 'liberal', as opposed to a 'conservative', is one who takes a generally activist view of the role of government, and who stresses the need for state-sponsored measures and programmes to realise economic goals including both prosperity and a fairer distribution of income and wealth.[3] By contrast, liberalism in the (longer-established) European sense is concerned with the realisation, enlargement and defence of individual freedom – of liberty; and a liberal is a person whose assessment of political and economic measures or systems is chiefly based on this concern.[4]

Freedom has an economic as well as a political dimension, and this has a number of aspects. It includes the freedom of people to spend their money as they wish, and to choose their lifestyles, occupations and places of work. For both individuals and business enterprises, it entails freedom to decide how and where to invest their time and resources, and which products and services to offer for sale on what terms. It implies the freedom to enter, for mutual benefit, into non-coercive arrangements and contracts of any kind, provided that these do not restrict the liberty of others. Further and not least, it embraces the right of people and businesses to move freely within national boundaries, and to choose where to live and operate. All this enters into the conception, not only of a free society, but also of a well-functioning market economy: the two are inseparable. Freedom of action for people and enterprises makes it possible for market initiatives to be taken and responses to be made, while these in turn provide the means through which

---

[3] For some American authors, it is a concern with fairness and equality that forms the defining characteristic of a 'liberal'. An example is Paul Krugman: 'I am a liberal - that is, I believe in a society that taxes the well-off and uses the proceeds to help the poor and unlucky.' (Paul Krugman, *Peddling Prosperity: Economic sense and nonsense in the age of diminished expectations*, New York: Norton, 1993.)

[4] There are three main references here, all of which deal with liberalism in general and economic liberalism in particular. First, there is F. A. Hayek's great treatise, *The Constitution of Liberty*, London: Routledge & Kegan Paul, 1960; second, Milton Friedman's *Capitalism and Freedom*, Chicago: Chicago University Press, 1962; and third and more recent, Samuel Brittan's *A Restatement of Economic Liberalism*, Basingstoke and London: Macmillan, 1988. The historical evolution of economic liberalism, both as doctrine and practice, is brilliantly treated in Joseph Schumpeter's *History of Economic Analysis*, London and New York: Oxford University Press, 1954.

preferences that are freely chosen and freely exercised can be given effect.[5]

Freedoms of this kind are a means as well as an end, since the operation of competitive markets makes economic systems less distorted, more responsive and more dynamic. Thus two widely accepted values, prosperity and individual liberty, are not only compatible but mutually supporting: this has been part of the representative economist's view of the world ever since Adam Smith advanced so brilliantly the thesis that the wealth of nations would be furthered by what he termed 'the system of natural liberty'.[6]

By the same token a free economy, because of its openness to change, brings with it elements of uncertainty and insecurity for which, in more regulated systems, various forms of insulation are available, at a cost (not always apparent) to others, for specially favoured categories or interests. Competitive markets are no respecters of status, hierarchy, established positions, or preconceived notions as to what particular roles, products or activities are worth; nor do they typically offer lifetime security of employment, except where this is provided for in freely negotiated contracts. Of course, people and enterprises are able to insure themselves against risks of various kinds: this is an integral part of a market system. All the same, there is an element of trade-off between economic freedom and prosperity, on the one hand, and on the other, making some aspects of the system more predictable by accepting or imposing restrictions on change and on adaptive responses to change. Job security in the former German Democratic Republic was greater than it has become since the unification of Germany.

The extension and exercise of economic freedoms make for closer *economic integration*, both within and across national boundaries. Viewed from this standpoint, liberalisation is a means

---

5 There is a useful listing of economic freedoms, set in the wider context of freedom in general, in Fritz Machlup's essay, 'Liberalism and the Choice of Freedoms', which forms a chapter in *Roads to Freedom: Essays in Honour of Friedrich A. von Hayek*, edited by Erich Streissler, London: Routledge & Kegan Paul, 1969.

6 The relationship between economic freedom and economic progress is explored further in the Annex (below, pp. 123-129).

to removing elements of disintegration within the system. Looking back, this is well illustrated by the series of measures taken by the governments of many continental European countries, in 'a shared historical transformation that lasted for over a century', to liberate the peasants from their former servile status. These actions established a new and open society 'in which all men were equal before the law, had freedom of movement and occupation, and were not bound by accident of birth to fixed social orders, each with its own privileges and responsibilities':[7] closer integration and the extension of economic freedoms went together. Within national states, and in groupings of states where free cross-border migration is permitted, full economic integration can be seen as a norm of liberalism.

Integration in this sense, which results from the opening up and operation of free markets, is not to be identified with uniformity: regulations which prescribe uniform standards, or uniform terms and conditions, may be a source of disintegration, through restricting the scope for enterprise and initiative and for mutually beneficial deals and contracts. Within the European Community, for example, the abolition of tariffs and other impediments to cross-border transactions has brought closer economic integration, but the provisions of the Social Chapter are likely to have the opposite effect.

Liberalism implies restricting the powers and functions of governments, so as to give full scope for individuals, families and enterprises: hence one of its leading principles is that of limited government, in the economic domain as elsewhere. At the same time, however, and contrary to what is often supposed, the liberal blueprint reserves an honoured place for the state, in economic as well as political life. For one thing, threats to the economic freedom of individuals and enterprises may arise, not just from governments, but also from restrictive or coercive behaviour by private persons and groups; and in using their powers in order to prevent or curtail such behaviour, governments can be a means to securing freedom. Historically, the most notable instances of this are the abolition of slavery and serfdom; but the same positive

---

[7] Jerome Blum, *The End of the Old Order in Rural Europe*, Princeton, NJ: Princeton University Press, 1978, pp. 8 and 377.

aspect is still relevant today – in particular, in the form of action to limit the abuse of market power by businesses, trade unions or professional groups. More broadly, the liberal blueprint assigns to governments an indispensable strategic role in establishing and maintaining a framework in which markets can function effectively, in particular through the definition and enforcement of property rights, and in making possible the provision of goods and services, such as national defence, which are collectively rather than individually consumed. This role is subject to continuous rethinking and revision as economic systems evolve, often in unforeseen ways, and new issues and problems arise: the recent crises in a number of East Asian countries, and the question of what lessons are to be drawn from them, provide a topical example which will be considered in Part 4 below. In countries such as Russia and the Ukraine today, the primary task is in fact to establish forms of government and an apparatus of public administration, together with norms and incentives for official and business behaviour, which will make it possible for the role of the state to be performed effectively. Liberalism is not anarchism, nor is it to be identified with unqualified *laissez-faire*.

This positive view of the state is consistent with the principle of limited government, for 'to limit the scope of an institution is not to reject it. Such limitation is calculated rather to strengthen it'.[8] Today as in the past, the authority of the state is weakened, rather than enhanced, when policies are decided with a view simply to placating particular interest groups, or when governments assume detailed commitments and responsibilities which they cannot effectively maintain. A captive state, or an overextended one, is not a strong state.

Liberalism is individualist, in that it defines the interests of national states, and the scope and purposes of government, with reference to the individuals who are subject to them: it is the welfare of people that counts. This however – and again, contrary to what is often suggested – does not imply that people act only

---

[8] Eli Heckscher, *Mercantilism*, London: Allen and Unwin, 1955; Vol. II, pp. 326-27. Heckscher makes the point that historically, in the early part of the 19th century, the reforms brought in by liberalism extended to government and public administration, with the aim of raising standards and enlarging the capacity of governments to act to good effect.

from selfish motives, nor that activities aside from market transactions are of little account. Again, it does not entail hostility towards co-operation, nor a failure to recognise the existence and value of institutions other than markets and states. 'The argument for liberty is not an argument against organisation', while 'The endeavour to achieve certain results by co-operation and organisation is as much a part of competition as individual efforts'.[9] It is only in so far as legally constituted groups and organisations act in such a way as to limit the freedom of others that their role is put in question. Subject to this, the principle of economic freedom clearly implies letting people decide for themselves the modes of action, whether individual or collective, that within the law will best suit their interests and obligations. Alongside it, the related principle of limited government likewise points away from centralisation and towards a readiness to make use of various levels of public administration. In both spheres, private and public, the liberal approach is pluralist. It opens the way to competition, variety and experiment in the choice and design of institutions.[10]

As with other such labels, economic liberalism is best thought of, not as a detailed creed or programme, but rather as a set of ideas and principles within which there may be many differences of view, a broad church sheltering a range of doctrines and beliefs.[11] The main single area of difference concerns the extent to which the redistribution of income and wealth should be viewed as an objective of government policy. One school of liberal thinking 'is appalled by the gross inequalities...in modern society', and holds that 'far-reaching direct fiscal measures should be taken by budgetary taxes and expenditures to moderate the high, and to

---

[9] Both quotations here are from Hayek, *The Constitution of Liberty*, *op. cit.*, p. 37.

[10] Critics of economic liberalism are apt to present it in crudely distorted terms. A recent instance is to be found in a book by an American geographer which refers to '...currently fashionable neo-conservative policy advocacies, with their glorification of privatized, atomistic competitive social relations and their signal and irrational aversion to anything that points in the direction of collective choice in economic matters'. (Allen J. Scott, *Regions and the World Economy: The Coming Shape of Global Production, Competition and Political Order*, New York: Oxford University Press, 1998, p. 162.)

[11] The point is developed well by Samuel Brittan, *A Restatement of Economic Liberalism*, *op. cit.*, pp. 75-77.

supplement the low, incomes and properties'.[12] By contrast, there is the perspective of Milton Friedman, and of Hayek too, in which an egalitarian approach is explicitly rejected. In Friedman's formulation:

> 'The egalitarian... will defend taking from some to give to others, not as a means by which the "some" can achieve an objective they want to achieve, but on grounds of "justice". At this point, equality comes sharply into conflict with freedom; one must choose. One cannot be both an egalitarian, in this sense, and a liberal.' [13]

It is true that, although philosophically there is a wide gap here, the extent of disagreement with respect to actual policies may not be great. Both egalitarians and non-egalitarians within the liberal camp want to minimise the degree to which redistributive measures impede the functioning of markets. More positively, both Friedman and Hayek, along with most of those who share their position, agree with the egalitarians on the need to guarantee some form of basic provision for all. Thus Friedman, though he would prefer a state of affairs in which this was made possible by private charity alone, has endorsed as a second-best the idea of a negative income tax as a means to ensuring a minimum money income for every citizen, while Hayek always accepted the principle of collective action to provide 'an assured minimum income... to all those who, for any reason, are not able to earn in the market an adequate maintenance'.[14] All the same, there are underlying differences here which cannot be papered over.

Questions of distribution and justice aside, there is a long list of other issues on which professed economic liberals may take different positions: current examples are the case for anti-trust

---

[12] The quotations are from James Meade, *The Intelligent Radical's Guide to Economic Policy*, London: Allen and Unwin, 1975.

[13] M. Friedman, *Capitalism and Freedom, op. cit.*, p. 163. Hayek made the same point in *The Constitution of Liberty* (p. 402): 'The liberal... is not an egalitarian'. By contrast, James Meade described himself (in the work just cited, p. 68) as 'an incurable egalitarian'.

[14] F.A. Hayek, *Law, Legislation and Liberty,* Vol. 2, *The Mirage of Social Justice*, London: Routledge & Kegan Paul, 1979, p. 87. To my mind this formula opens the door to a possibly wide range of discretionary redistributive measures, since it is not the case that a more or less uniform class of 'deserving poor' can readily be identified and made subject to standard forms and conditions of assistance. Hayek's wording glosses over what has always been, and remains, a major problem for liberalism.

policies, the design of prudential regulations for financial markets and institutions, the merits of different exchange rate régimes, the uses of international economic co-operation, and (though this is less actively debated) the legalisation of drugs.[15] Both the issues themselves and the arguments relating to them are subject to continual reshaping as a result of new developments on the economic and political scene: the most recent instance of this is the current world-wide debate on the possible need for closer regulation of banks and financial markets and of international short-term capital flows – or more broadly, for international co-operative action to contain the risks of contagious financial instability or world-wide deflation.

Given the differences of opinion among liberals, their shared recognition of a central and positive role for government, and the need in any case to re-examine this role as circumstances change, the fortunes of economic liberalism are not always and necessarily to be identified with what Margaret Thatcher termed 'rolling back the frontiers of the state'. All the same, such a rolling back has been the dominant aspect of this recent phase of economic reform, simply because of the extent to which interventionism prevailed in most countries of the world at the time that the present story begins, towards the end of the 1970s.

Background and Point of Departure

From the end of the Second World War to the close of the 1970s – and indeed, until well into the 1980s – the summary history of economic policies across the world can be presented in terms of three groups of countries. The first group is made up of what I term the core OECD countries – that is, the 24 countries which throughout these past 20 years, and indeed before then, were members of the Organisation for Economic Co-operation and Development.[16] The second and numerically largest group consists

---

[15] This last question is considered in Richard Stevenson, *Winning the War on Drugs: To Legalise or Not?*, Hobart Paper No. 124, London: Institute of Economic Affairs, 1994.

[16] From the early 1970s up to 1994, the membership of the OECD remained unchanged at 24 countries, while the question of new accessions was not on the agenda. This 'core' membership comprised 19 European countries – the 15 countries that are now members of the European Community, plus Iceland, Norway, Switzerland and Turkey – together with the USA, Canada, Japan, Australia and New Zealand. Since 1994 five more countries –

of the developing countries including China, while the third comprises the former communist countries of Central and Eastern Europe and what was then the Soviet Union.

In the latter case, there is not much of a background story to tell. Despite a few experiments in reform here and there, the governments of the communist countries retained their commitment to the ultimate goal of a marketless, fully-planned economy, while in practice their economic systems remained highly regulated and controlled. In the other two groups of countries, however, the balance between liberalism and interventionism changed significantly, over these three decades or more, in ways that differed over different areas of policy as well as across frontiers.

Contrasting Views of the Years following World War II

For the core OECD countries, a general assessment for the period as a whole depends on how divergent tendencies within them are to be compared and weighed. This is illustrated in the contrasting views of history taken by two distinguished economists within the liberal camp. Terence Hutchison, in an essay first published in 1979, argued that

> 'So persistent, and seemingly ineluctable, has been the expansion of the role of government in so many economically advanced, democratic countries, that it is difficult to cite any case from such countries where a significant rolling back of the interventionist tide has been achieved, *except after major wars*. Even here, the role of government has usually been reduced only as compared with the all-pervasive control and regulation of wartime, and not nearly pushed back to the previous peacetime level.'[17]

By contrast, Gottfried Haberler, writing some years later but referring to the same sequence of events, took the view that, while at the end of the Second World War 'faith in capitalism and free markets was at an all-time low', the eclipse of economic liberalism was short-lived. A turning point came with the radical economic

---

Mexico, the Czech Republic, Poland, Hungary and the Republic of Korea – have been admitted to membership.

[17] Terence Hutchison, *The Politics and Philosophy of Economics*, Oxford: Blackwell, 1981, p. 160; the italics are in the original. The text goes on: 'To these generalizations the Social-Market Economy of the German Federal Republic has provided the outstanding exception.'

reforms of 1948 in West Germany, soon followed by similar measures in some neighbouring European countries. Subsequently, this momentum was broadly maintained: 'There has been some backsliding in a few countries, but by and large economic liberalism has progressed in the western world.'[18]

These assessments conflict because the authors are implicitly focusing on different aspects of economic policy. Hutchison's sombre verdict takes too little account of the remarkable extent to which the core OECD countries generally, and the European members in particular, liberalised cross-border transactions over the years from 1947 onwards. Here there were four main elements. *First*, the elaborate structures of quota restrictions on imports which the European countries had built up were largely dismantled during the late 1940s and early 1950s, while most Japanese import quotas were likewise removed over the 1960s. *Second*, there were dramatic advances towards free trade within Western Europe, chiefly through the formation of the European Economic Community and the European Free Trade Area. *Third*, all the OECD countries, apart from Australia, New Zealand and Turkey, accepted and applied the multilaterally agreed reductions in tariffs that emerged from successive negotiating rounds in the General Agreement on Tariffs and Trade (the GATT). *Fourth*, by the end of the 1950s almost all these countries had introduced current account convertibility of their currencies; and in 1961 they established within the OECD itself the Codes of Liberalisation of Capital Movements and Invisible Transactions as a mechanism for progressively freeing transactions under both these heads, while over time the scope of these Codes was extended. It is true that most countries retained exchange controls, and that in all of them there remained strong elements of trade protectionism which in some ways, in both Europe and North America, were actually reinforced as time went on. But over the OECD area as a whole, the record of external liberalisation was impressive and its effects wide-ranging.

On the other hand, Haberler's favourable assessment of the period may have given too little weight to counter-liberal

---

[18] Gottfried Haberler, *International Trade and Economic Development*, San Francisco: International Center for Economic Growth, 1988, pp. 2 and 3.

tendencies which became clearly apparent in most OECD national economies. One of these was the extension of public ownership of business enterprises, notably through the programmes of nationalisation that were carried through in the post-war years in Britain, France and some other European countries. A second was the general and continuing rise of public expenditure, and hence taxation, in relation to GDP.[19] It is true that, strictly speaking, neither the extent of public ownership nor the ratio of public expenditure to GDP need be good measures of the degree of departure from liberal norms. In both cases, much may depend on how far they are associated with constraints on the operation of markets, and this can vary from case to case and over time.[20] For public enterprises, practice has differed widely: at the one extreme they have been set up as government departments, with close political control and no systematic concern with profitability, while at the other, they have been allowed or instructed to act in much the same way as private businesses. Again, in interpreting public expenditure ratios, allowance should ideally be made for 'tax expenditures' – that is, special tax exemptions, allowances, credits and reliefs – which have much the same effects as grants or subsidies but do not appear as such and are harder to identify and measure: to focus on expenditures alone gives an incomplete picture of the extent of interventionism. All the same, there is a clear presumption that both privatisation and reductions in high public expenditure ratios, such as those that now prevail in most of the OECD area, will bring economic systems closer to the liberal blueprint.

Whether the economies of the core OECD countries as a group were on balance freer at the beginning of the 1970s than they had been 25 years earlier is perhaps debatable. My own view is that Haberler is closer to the mark than Hutchison; and in any case, it is too unqualified to hold, as Yergin and Stanislaw do, that 'Overall,

---

[19] Evidence on the long-run growth of public expenditures, and an assessment of its effects, is to be found in Vito Tanzi and Ludger Schuknecht, 'The Growth of Government and the Reform of the State in Industrial Countries', IMF Working Paper 95/130.

[20] In Britain, for example, systematic attempts were made in the 1960s, notably through the White Papers of 1961 and 1967, to make nationalised industries more commercially oriented and less subject to discretionary pressures from governments. Despite what proved to be their limitations as such, these were moves towards liberalisation.

the advance of state control seemed to be inexorable', and that the changes brought in by the British Labour government of 1945 'marked the beginning of an economic and political tide that reached its peak in the 1970s'.[21]

The 1970s: Liberalism in Retreat

Whatever the verdict on the post-war decades, there is no doubt that in most if not all of these countries the early and mid-1970s brought a decline in the fortunes of economic liberalism. This mainly resulted from the serious and unexpected worsening of the economic situation which occurred in virtually all the group – with slower rates of growth in output and trade and higher rates of both inflation and unemployment. Harassed governments responded with a range of interventionist measures, which included controls on prices and wages, intergovernmental deals and state-directed programmes in energy markets, bailing out (in some cases through nationalisation) of loss-making firms and industries, increasing resort to highly illiberal forms of trade protection including in particular (so-called) voluntary export restraint agreements, closer restrictions on inward direct investment, and tighter foreign exchange controls. At the same time, there was a general failure to trim public expenditure programmes in response to the now substantially lower rates of growth: hence government spending rose further, in many cases sharply, in relation to GDP. As usual, the evolution of policies was neither straightforward nor consistent, and one could compile for the period a list of liberalising measures for most of these countries. But the trend was in the opposite direction: a shift towards interventionism came through a complex of reactions, not always fully intended or worked out in advance, to situations, problems and crises which few had foreseen.

The Developing World

In the developing countries, generally speaking, both the prevailing official philosophy and the trend of economic policies were

---

[21] D. Yergin and J. Stanislaw, *The Commanding Heights*, *op. cit.*, pp. 11 and 21. The authors also assert, mistakenly, that 'the late nineteenth-century world' was 'a world of expanding economic opportunity and ever-diminishing barriers to travel and trade' (p. 16). Though the international economic system of June 1914 was a liberal one, arguably more so than that of today, barriers to trade notably increased from 1879 onwards.

interventionist right through the decades following the Second World War. Outside Latin America and East Asia, almost all governments were consciously and explicitly socialist, so that the extension of public ownership and state direction, and restrictions on the freedom of action of private investors, were largely taken for granted. Almost everywhere it was believed that investment programmes should be planned from the centre, and that the development of industry required general protection against imports, together with promotion by governments of specific industries and projects. In many cases, the emergence of balance-of-payments problems led to the imposition of quantitative import restrictions, which were later retained or intensified. Strict exchange controls and close regulation of private inward direct investment were almost universal. Not only did the developing countries stand aside from the GATT agreements which brought multilateral reductions in trade barriers, but those of them who were prepared to join the GATT negotiated in the 1960s a special status which largely exempted them from the restraints and obligations that went with normal membership and were accepted, though not always fully honoured, by the core OECD countries.

There were some exceptions to this general pattern. Both Hong Kong and Singapore established trade régimes which were actually more open than those of the core OECD countries. From the early 1960s, as a result of policy changes, 'Overall protection for industry was zero for Korea and low for Taiwan',[22] while Malaysia adopted a fairly open trade régime. The Indonesian economy became less highly regulated after the Sukarno régime was brought to an end in 1966. More broadly, public expenditure ratios everywhere in the group as a whole were and remained low by the standards of almost all the core OECD countries. But for the most part, although there was greater diversity among them, the economic systems of the developing countries became more regulated and less market-oriented than those of the OECD members.

As in the OECD area, economic policy régimes in most of the group became more interventionist during the early to mid-1970s –

---

[22] Ian M. D. Little, *Economic Development: Theory, Policy and International Relations*, New York: Basic Books, 1982, p. 141.

31

though not for the same reasons, since generally speaking the economic situation and performance of these countries did not worsen in the same disconcerting way. There were numerous further expropriations of foreign-owned oil companies and mining operations. Protectionism and 'insulationism' became more firmly entrenched, and governments collectively, in the so-called 'Group of 77', put a lot of wasted diplomatic energy into arguing for the 'new international economic order' programme which rested on a wholly non-liberal conception of the working of the international system. Within individual countries, there were notable counter-liberal initiatives, including large extensions of public ownership in India and the adoption of a new and highly interventionist industrial strategy in Korea. In China, these were the final years of the Cultural Revolution. Only in Chile, after the overthrow of the Allende régime in 1973, did economic policies begin to move decisively in the opposite direction.

A Low Point, then a Turn of the Tide

By the mid-to-late 1970s, therefore, the fortunes of economic liberalism across the world, in all the main country groupings, were at a low ebb. This was true not only of events, but also of ideas, perceptions and convictions. As compared with the 'golden age' of 1950-73, there had been an obvious falling away in performance in the market economies of the core OECD countries, as opposed to the rest of the world including, as it then appeared, the socialist countries. This was widely taken as evidence of the basic weakness of capitalism and of market-directed economic systems.

It is from the late 1970s that signs begin to show of a new shift in the balance, a reversal of the counter-liberal tide. Although as usual in economic history there is no dramatic turning point, I would myself choose 1978 as the year of transition. Within the OECD group, member governments collectively resolved to take steps to free their oil markets. The OECD Ministerial Communiqué of that year referred to the need to raise prices of energy products to world levels, and in a special annex on 'positive adjustment' it endorsed the principle of 'relying as much as possible on market forces to encourage mobility of labour and capital to their most productive uses'. In the US, far-reaching measures of industry deregulation were adopted, in airlines and road freight transport;

and in China, the government inaugurated the historic change 'to a cautious pragmatic reformism which relaxed central political control and modified the economic system profoundly'.[23] In terms of personalities, the odd couple of Deng Xiaoping and Alfred Kahn[24] appear as leading (though of course unconnected) figures in the advance guard of world reformers. In May 1979, as a result of the then general election in Britain, they were joined by Margaret Thatcher, and a few months later her government announced the suspension of the United Kingdom's comprehensive and long-established system of exchange controls. These were early indications of a trend which, despite initial limitations and some further local reverses, has since been largely maintained and extended over the world as a whole.

---

[23] Angus Maddison, *Chinese Economic Performance in the Long Run*, Paris: OECD Development Centre, 1998, p.55.

[24] Kahn, a professor of economics, was then Secretary of Transportation in the US, in the Democratic administration headed by President Carter. He was a moving force in deregulation in the US.

Part 2: The Uneasy Trend to Economic Liberalism

IN RELATION TO THESE PAST TWO DECADES, I offer three overlapping sketches of the evolution of economic policies.

A General View Across the World

First, I draw on the extensive evidence on liberalisation which is to be found in the latest report of the 'Economic Freedom of the World' project.[25] This provides 'economic freedom ratings' over the period 1975-95 for 115 countries. The ratings are on a numerical scale which goes from zero to a maximum of 10, and bring together a range of indicators. In most cases, ratings are given for 1975, 1980, 1985, 1990 and 1995, though there are some gaps for the earlier years. Understandably, there are still areas of policy that are not fully covered by the ratings, while in a number of cases the interpretation they give of developments in particular countries is open to question. In any case, such indicators at best provide only part of the story.[26] However, I believe that the broad impression of change that the figures convey is accurate enough for them to be used here. I have therefore taken the ratings as a basis for constructing three summary tables of my own. Together these offer a preliminary general view of the reform process as a whole, and of the varying extent of liberalisation as between different countries and country groupings.

Reformers and Non-Reformers

In Table 1 I classify all but one of the 115 countries into three groups: reforming, where the rating has increased; counter-reforming, where the extent of economic freedom has apparently diminished; and intermediate, where there has been little change or no clear trend.[27] In this last category, where there was no definite

---

[25] James Gwartney and Robert Lawson, *Economic Freedom of the World 1997: Annual Report,* Vancouver, BC: Fraser Institute, 1997.

[26] A brief review of the ratings and their significance is given in the Annex to this Paper.

[27] The country excluded is Hong Kong. This consistently receives the highest rating which remains unchanged throughout the period. Hence the series is trendless; but even so, it

Table 1: 1975-1995: The Geography of Economic Reform

| Country Grouping | Number of Countries | | | |
	Reforming	Intermediate	Counter-Reforming	Total
Core OECD	23	-	-	23
Asian countries	13	1	-	14
Non-OECD Europe	11	5	-	16
Latin America	15	4	4	23
Sub-total	62	10	4	76
African continent & Middle East	15	15	8	38
Total	77	25	12	114

Source: J. Gwartney and R. Lawson, *Economic Freedom of the World, 1997: Annual Report.*

tendency over the period as a whole, there are 25 countries. Of the remaining 89 countries for which a trend is apparent, or where a decisive recent move has been made, 77 appear as having liberalised on balance, while only 12 have moved in the opposite direction.

In one respect, these figures may somewhat overstate the predominance of the reformers, since among the countries excluded for want of data there are several which, even in the absence of a numerical rating, can be classed as non-reforming: examples are Afghanistan, Belarus, Cambodia, Cuba, Iraq, Liberia, Libya, Myanmar and Sudan. As against this, however, and much more significant, the figures in Table 1 greatly understate the extent to which liberalisation has been the prevailing tendency, because they count each country as one regardless of size. In practice, the non-reforming countries are not only in the minority but also, generally speaking, of relatively small economic weight. If, for example, we

would be misleading to classify so liberal a régime among the non-reformers.

take the 12 counter-reformers, their combined GDP for 1990, as given in a recent study by Angus Maddison,[28] was less than 10 per cent higher than the corresponding figure for Canada. The largest national economy within this group is that of Iran, which in 1990 had a GDP less than that of the Netherlands. Among the 25 intermediate countries, the largest to be included in Maddison's tables is Nigeria, with a GDP figure for 1990 which slightly exceeded that of Denmark. The combined 1990 GDP for all the 37 non-reformers taken together is probably not much greater than that of France, while the 77 countries classed here as reforming account for well over 90 per cent of total world GDP.

The ratio of reformers to non-reformers differs considerably as between different groups of countries: this also appears from Table 1, where five groupings are shown. *First*, there are 23 of the core OECD economies (Luxembourg is not covered in the study). All of these can be classed as reformist – even though, as will be seen, some of them appear as distinctly lukewarm. *Second* come 14 Asian countries, including China (but not Japan, which is included under OECD). Here all but one count as reformers: the exception is Nepal, which appears as intermediate. A *third* group comprises 16 countries from central and eastern Europe including Russia. Of these, several are arguably borderline or still-uncertain cases. I have classified 11 as reformers and five (Cyprus, Albania, Croatia, Romania and Ukraine) as intermediate; here again, there are no counter-reformers. *Fourth*, there are 23 countries in Latin America and the Caribbean. Of these, four only appear as counter-reformers: the largest of these is Venezuela, with a 1992 GDP, in Maddison's estimates, roughly equal to that of Belgium, while the others are Haiti, Honduras and (more debatably) Nicaragua. There are also four Latin American or Caribbean countries, all of them small, which appear as intermediate. The reformers here comprise 15 of the 23 countries, including the three largest economies of the region – Brazil, Mexico and Argentina.

Taking these four groupings together, there are 62 countries classed as reforming, including all the 20 largest national economies within the whole set of 114, 10 intermediate cases, and

[28] Angus Maddison, *Monitoring the World Economy, 1820-1992*, Paris: OECD Development Centre, 1995.

only four counter-reformers. This leaves 38 countries in Africa and the Middle East, and here the balance is different. Only 15 of these countries count as reformers, and some of these, as will be seen, have not moved very far down the path of liberalisation. Another 15 countries appear as intermediate,[29] and eight as counter-reformers. Besides Iran, this latter category comprises Algeria, Syria, and five countries in sub-Saharan Africa including the Democratic Republic of the Congo (formerly Zaire), Cameroon and Zimbabwe.

On this evidence, therefore, a clear trend towards liberalisation is to be seen in every core OECD country, and in many if not most countries outside this group including the largest economies among them. Across Europe, the American continent and much of Asia, it is the non-reformers that are exceptional.

The Extent of Reform

Of course, this is only the beginning of the story: it has to be asked how far liberalisation has actually been taken in the various countries that are classed here as reforming. Evidence on this, likewise derived from the economic freedom ratings, is presented in Tables 2 and 3.

First, by combining the country ratings, using Maddison's 1990 GDP estimates as country weights,[30] I have constructed a similar 'index of economic freedom' for the five country groupings and the world as a whole over the period 1975-95. These series are shown in Table 2, which covers 61 countries including Hong Kong: the other 54 countries are left out for reasons of smallness of size or deficiencies of data.

It can be seen that for the world as a whole the progress of reform appears halting over the period 1975-85: modest increases in the ratings for the core OECD countries and Asia are partly

---

[29] However, a recent publication from the International Monetary Fund suggests that as a result of recent policy changes two countries from this intermediate category, Benin and Cote d'Ivoire, can now be included among the reformers. (S. Fischer, E. Hernandez-Cata and M.S. Khan, *Africa: Is This the Turning Point?*, Washington, DC: International Monetary Fund, 1998.)

[30] For Russia, the GDP figure is taken from Maddison's 'The Nature and Functioning of European Capitalism: A Historical and Comparative Perspective', published by the Groningen Growth and Development Centre, 1997.

Table 2: Combined Economic Freedom Ratings, 1975-95

	1975	1980	1985	1990	1995
Core OECD countries (22)	5.3	5.5	5.8	6.6	7.0
Asia (13)	3.1	3.4	3.7	4.5	5.0
Latin America (7)	4.0	3.6	3.4	4.3	4.9
Africa & Middle East (14)	3.5	3.0	3.3	3.6	3.8
Central & Eastern Europe (5)	1.0	2.0	1.6	1.7	3.9
World Total (61 countries)	4.5	4.6	4.8	5.6	6.1

Notes and Sources: The economic freedom ratings for individual countries are from *Economic Freedom of the World, 1997*, except for a few cases in 1975 where I made my own assumptions to fill gaps in the series. I have combined the individual figures into regional and world totals by weighting them on the basis of estimated 1990 GDP, as given by Angus Maddison in the sources quoted in the main text. The respective percentage weights for the five country groupings are: core OECD countries, 59.7; Asia, 24.9; Latin America, 7.6; Africa & Middle East, 3.6; and Central & Eastern Europe, 4.2.

offset by contrary tendencies elsewhere. For the decade 1985-95 there is a relatively small rise for Africa and the Middle East; but the other four groups, and hence the index for the world as a whole, all show more substantial increases. For both the core OECD countries and Asia there is a fairly steady upward trend over the whole 20 years. In the Latin American region, on this evidence, liberalisation gets under away only from the mid-1980s, while in central and eastern Europe, as one would expect, it is only after 1990 that the effects of economic reform begin to show.

The ratings can also be used to throw light on the comparative extent to which reform has been taken in different reforming countries: this is shown in Table 3. The Table presents figures for 54 out of the 77 countries identified as reformers: here again, the smaller countries are largely excluded, except for a few cases where the extent of change is striking.

The last two columns of Table 3 provide alternative measures of the extent to which reform has been taken in each country during the period 1975-95. The penultimate column shows the absolute increases in freedom ratings, comparing each country's 1995 rating with an initial figure defined as the lowest for any of the earlier years covered in the study. The initial year can therefore be 1975, 1980, 1985 or 1990, and is shown in the Table in brackets. Judged by this measure, the top 10 reformers, in descending order, are New Zealand, Mauritius and Chile, Iceland and Argentina, Peru and Portugal, Poland, and the Philippines and Jamaica. Three notable late starters, where significant increases were realised over the period 1990-95, are the Czech Republic, Russia and Hungary.

The figures in the final column of the Table, which are my own, offer a ranking which allows for the cross-country differences in initial pre-reform situations. The more regulated a country was initially, the greater the scope for reform. Hence this measure takes into account not only the extent of reform, as shown in the penultimate column, but how this relates to what could in principle have been achieved, given the point of departure: the reforming countries are ranked by relating the absolute increases in their ratings to the potential for reform at the time when liberalisation was begun. The potential is given by the difference between the initial rating, as defined above, and the maximum rating which is 10.

The cases of Portugal and South Korea, which appear with equal ranking in the 13th and 14th rows of Table 3, will serve as illustrations. For Portugal, the lowest rating, of 2.5, was for 1975. This is taken as the point of departure, when the potential was 7.5. Over the period to 1995 the rating increased by 3.4, from 2.5 to 5.9. Expressing this increase as a percentage of the scope for reform, the initial potential of 7.5, yields the figure of 45 per cent which appears in the final column. South Korea, for which the point of departure is 1980, gets the same percentage, and therefore the same ranking, despite the fact that the increase in its rating from 1980 to 1995 is lower at 2.7, because its initial potential was less than that of Portugal.[31]

---

[31] A third possible comparison would be to take direct proportionate changes in the ratings. This would yield a quite different set of rankings, in which a low initial starting point, other things being equal, gave countries a higher rather than a lower comparative figure. For example, in the case of the two countries just referred to, the increase for Portugal would then be 136 per cent, as compared with 67.5 per cent for South Korea.

Table 3: Changes in Economic Freedom Ratings for 54 Reforming Countries, 1975–95

	Country	Rating Initial	Rating (year)	Rating 1995	Change Absolute	Change % of initial scope for reform
1	New Zealand	4.1	(1985)	8.0	3.9	66
2	Mauritius	3.9	(1980)	7.6	3.7	61
3	Chile	2.7	(1975)	6.4	3.7	51
4	Iceland	2.9	(1980)	6.5	3.6	51
5	Argentina	2.8	(1985)	6.4	3.6	50
6	UK	4.6	(1980)	7.3	2.7	50
7	Singapore	6.4	(1975)	8.2	1.8	50
8	Philippines	4.1	(1975)	7.0	2.9	49
9	Peru	2.9	(1985)	6.3	3.4	48
10	Costa Rica	4.5	(1985)	7.1	2.6	47
11	Thailand	4.8	(1975)	7.2	2.4	46
12	USA	6.1	(1975)	7.9	1.8	46
13	Portugal	2.5	(1975)	5.9	3.4	45
14	South Korea	4.0	(1980)	6.7	2.7	45
15	Norway	3.3	(1980)	6.1	2.8	42
16	Jamaica	3.0	(1980)	5.9	2.9	41
17	Ireland	4.1	(1975)	6.5	2.4	41
18	Australia	5.0	(1975)	7.0	2.2	40
19	France	3.6	(1985)	6.1	2.5	39
20	Taiwan	4.8	(1975)	6.8	2.0	38
21	Czech Republic	2.4	(1990)	5.2	2.8	37
22	Sweden	3.5	(1980)	5.9	2.4	37
23	Mexico	3.8	(1980)	6.1	2.3	37
24	Finland	3.9	(1975)	6.1	2.2	36
25	Poland	1.2	(1985)	4.3	3.1	35
26	Denmark	3.7	(1985)	5.9	2.2	35
27	Malaysia	5.4	(1975)	7.0	1.6	35
28	Israel	2.0	(1975)	4.6	2.6	33
29	Sri Lanka	3.4	(1980)	5.6	2.2	33
30	Spain	3.9	(1975)	5.9	2.0	33
31	Japan	5.1	(1975)	6.7	1.6	33

32	Tanzania	2.1	(1985)	4.6	2.5	32
33	South Africa	3.8	(1975)	5.7	1.9	31
34	Hungary	3.0	(1990)	5.1	2.1	30
35	Kenya	3.3	(1975)	5.3	2.0	30
36	Colombia	3.6	(1980)	5.5	1.9	30
37	Italy	3.6	(1985)	5.5	1.9	30
38	Indonesia	4.7	(1980)	6.3	1.6	30
39	Russia	0.9	(1990)	3.5	2.6	29
40	Turkey	2.3	(1980)	4.5	2.2	29
41	Pakistan	2.6	(1975)	4.6	2.0	27
42	China	2.3	(1980)	4.3	2.0	26
43	Ghana	2.5	(1980)	4.4	1.9	25
44	Greece	3.3	(1985)	5.0	1.7	25
45	Austria	4.7	(1980)	6.0	1.3	25
46	Egypt	2.1	(1975)	4.0	1.9	24
47	Canada	5.9	(1985)	6.9	1.0	24
48	Netherlands	5.5	(1980)	6.5	1.0	22
49	Bangladesh	2.8	(1980)	4.2	1.4	19
50	Brazil	2.3	(1985)	3.7	1.4	18
51	India	3.3	(1975)	4.4	1.1	16
52	Belgium	5.6	(1975)	6.3	0.7	16
53	Switzerland	7.0	(1975)	7.4	0.4	13
54	Germany	5.9	(1975)	6.4	0.5	12

Source: J. Gwartney and R. Lawson, *Economic Freedom of the World, 1997: Annual Report, op. cit.*

From this final column of Table 3, New Zealand appears as clearly the leading reformer, with Mauritius unchallenged in second place. After that the percentages fall away gradually; and in any case, no great significance should be attached to the exact rankings. However, it is worth noting that in the top third of the table, where the countries have a comparative rating of 40 per cent or more, 10 of the 18 countries come from outside the core OECD group. Apart from Mauritius, all of these are either from Asia (Singapore, the Philippines, Thailand and South Korea) or from Latin America where Chile and Argentina are the leaders. Of the largest OECD economies which form the G7 grouping, only two appear in this top echelon – the UK and the US, in that order.

In the next 20 countries, where the percentages range from 30 to 39, there are three countries from sub-Saharan Africa (Tanzania, South Africa and Kenya) and three from central and eastern Europe (the Czech Republic, Poland and Hungary). Three of the G7 members – France, Japan and Italy – also fall into this group, as do Mexico, Taiwan and Malaysia.

Finally, the 16 countries with percentages below 30 include several core OECD members. Most of these had high initial ratings but have since, it would seem, made only limited further moves towards reform. This description fits Austria, Canada and the Netherlands, and even more so Belgium, Switzerland and Germany which appear at the bottom of the list: indeed, from the evidence of Table 3 alone, one might question the claims of these three latter countries to be classed among the reformers. Also in this lowest section of Table 3 is a group of countries whose economies were highly regulated at the time when the reforming process first set in, which have indeed been subject to limited reforms, but where liberalisation has still a long way to go: here the only core OECD member is Turkey. The group includes Russia, China, India, Bangladesh, Egypt and Brazil.

Groups of Countries and Areas of Policy

Moving beyond the 'Economic Freedom of the World' estimates, the recent story of reform can also be told with reference to the three groups of countries identified above and seven partly overlapping areas of policy. These areas are (i) financial markets, (ii) international transactions, including both trade and capital flows, (iii) corporatisation, privatisation and deregulation of industries, (iv) energy policies, (v) agricultural policies, (vi) labour markets, and (vii) public finance.[32]

Looking first at the 24 countries of the core OECD group, four main aspects of liberalisation stand out.[33]

---

[32] This is both a narrower and a wider range than that of the 'Economic Freedom of the World' study - narrower, in that the study covers also macro-economic policies in each country and the extent to which inflation has been curbed, but wider, in that it does not as yet include developments in labour markets and does not cover the agriculture or energy sectors as such.

[33] The following summary draws in particular on a range of OECD reports, including country economic surveys, many of which are not quoted directly or cited.

To start with, there are two related areas of policy in which radical reforms have been made, with the effect in particular of bringing economies which were initially highly regulated into line with those which had liberalised already – and which themselves, in almost every case, have now moved further still. These two areas are *financial markets* and *cross-border capital flows* including direct foreign investment. Here the most restrictive countries initially fell into three groups: France and Southern Europe, the Nordic countries apart from Denmark, and Australia and New Zealand. Now all these countries have abolished exchange controls, made foreign investment flows, inward and outward, far less subject to regulation than was the case, for many of them, 15 or 20 years ago, and deregulated, in many instances substantially, domestic financial markets. Not surprisingly, there is still scope for the further opening up of financial markets to competition, while most if not all core OECD countries still have residual restrictions on direct foreign investment. Even so, in these areas of policy the scene has been transformed.

Privatisation and Deregulation

A notable development, which initially was novel and surprising, has been *privatisation*. In this, the British government elected in 1979 was the forerunner within the OECD group and a leading practitioner throughout. Privatisation has proved to be a far-reaching and truly innovative line of reform, which has spread to every part of the world. At the same time, there has been a clear and widespread trend, in a number of sectors of the economy, towards *deregulation*: this has made for freer entry into the industries concerned, and widened the scope for competition both within and across national boundaries. The industries chiefly affected have been financial services, transport, telecommunications, and power generation. The main heads of action have been opening up licensing arrangements so as to increase the extent of competition, allowing private competition in markets which had formerly been reserved for public monopoly enterprises, and dismantling of statutory controls over prices and entry.[34]

---

[34] OECD, *Assessing Structural Reform: Lessons for the Future*, Paris: OECD, 1994, p. 9.

Privatisation can take various forms, and some of these, by limiting the extent to which competition is made possible, are less market-oriented than others. For example, the British Gas Corporation was sold in 1986 with its monopoly powers still substantially intact, while the rules governing the initial privatisations in France in 1986-88 were specifically designed to restrict the scope for foreign ownership of the assets sold. Over time, however, there has been a clear tendency to move in the direction of greater liberalism and more open arrangements, whether in the initial choice of methods of privatisation or through subsequent action to promote competition and freer entry in industries that have been privatised. In this area, therefore, despite the various and often considerable limitations that still remain on the extent to which competition and free entry prevail, liberalisation has gone further than the story of the transfer of ownership might in itself suggest.

On deregulation, however, there is another side to the picture. How far there has been a general trend towards less regulated economies over the OECD area, looking at economic systems as a whole as distinct from particular industries, is debatable. In an OECD Secretariat report published last year, which uses a threefold classification of government regulations into economic, social and administrative, the statement is made that 'social and administrative regulations... are expanding rapidly in OECD countries'.[35] In a recent review article, John Taylor summarised developments in the US during the 1970s and the 1980s as embodying 'conflicting trends...: increasing social regulation with inadequate attention to cost-benefit analysis and other economic considerations compared with decreasing economic regulation...'.[36] This broad generalisation probably holds good for other core OECD countries in relation to the past decade or more. It is indeed probable that, outside the deregulated industries listed above, a typical business enterprise in many if not most core OECD countries is more closely regulated

---

[35] OECD, *Report on Regulatory Reform: Synthesis*, Paris: OECD, 1997, p.7.

[36] John B. Taylor, 'Changes in American Economic Policy in the 1980s: Watershed or Pendulum Swing?', *Journal of Economic Literature*, Vol. XXXIII, No. 2, June 1995, p.782. The book under review was Martin Feldstein (ed.), *American Economic Policy in the 1980s*, University of Chicago Press, 1994.

now than was the case 20 years ago, as a result of the increasing impact of regulations, whether specific or economy-wide, relating to (in particular) the environment, occupational health and safety, the tax régime, and – as will be seen below – the freedom to hire.

The Freeing of International Trade

A *third* area of reform has been *trade liberalisation* Although the core OECD countries are still a long way from endorsing free trade,[37] they have made substantial moves in that direction. In some instances, notably Japan, Australia, New Zealand and Turkey, liberalisation has in part been unilateral. But the main developments in the group have taken place through regional and multilateral agreements. Under the regional heading, there have been the Closer Economic Relations Agreement of 1983 between Australia and New Zealand; the enlargement of the European Community and the establishment within it of the Single Market, together with the formation of the European Economic Area; and the association of Canada and the US, with the later accession of Mexico, in what is now the North American Free Trade Agreement. Although there is room for debate here, my own view is that up to now these various regional integration agreements have served on balance to further the cause of cross-border liberalisation in the world as a whole.[38]

Within the European Community, the decision of member governments in 1985 to proceed with the creation of the Single Market was a landmark event. The Single Market Programme has had both an external and an internal dimension. As to the former, it provided for the phasing out of all remaining national (as distinct from Community-wide) restrictions on trade in goods. Its main

---

[37] It is true that, in a White Paper issued in November 1996, the then British government formally endorsed the goal of global free trade by 2020 (Foreign and Commonwealth Office and Department of Trade and Industry, *Free Trade and Foreign Policy: A Global Vision*, London: Stationery Office, 1996). However, a different government has since come into office, and in any case the external trade régime of the UK has long been, with a few residual qualifications, the régime of the European Community as a whole.

[38] This was the judgement of a WTO Secretariat study published a few years ago: 'To a much greater extent than is often acknowledged, regional and multilateral integration initiatives are complements rather than alternatives in the pursuit of more open trade.' (*Regionalism and the World Trading System*, Geneva: WTO, 1995, p.3.)

effects, however, have been to liberalise further cross-border transactions of all kinds within the Community itself. In relation to one another, member countries bound themselves to free both public procurement and trade in services; to establish free movement of both capital flows and persons; and to have regard to the principle of 'mutual recognition' of rules and standards, rather than trying to agree in every case on full and detailed harmonisation which (as seen above) may have disintegrating effects. Although the stated aims of the programme are still some way from being realised, it has brought notable advances towards closer economic integration within the Community.

As to the multilateral aspects of freer international trade, the outstanding event has been the liberalisation eventually agreed to in 1994, admittedly at the end of a long and hard road and with many limitations, as a result of the Uruguay Round negotiations. Since the conclusion of the Uruguay Round agreement, some progress has been made in giving effect to its provisions, and in providing for further liberalisation within the World Trade Organization (WTO), as in the recent multilateral agreements relating to information technology, telecommunications, and financial services. The decision to replace the GATT, which had functioned since 1947, with the newly-constituted WTO which has wider terms of reference, greater powers and a more assured status, is itself evidence that member countries are concerned to strengthen the multilateral trade and investment system and the rules, understandings and procedures that support it. One expert commentator, John Jackson, has suggested that the establishment of the WTO marks 'a watershed in the international system', since the creation of 'a definitive international arrangement' has gone together with a remarkable expansion in the range of topics that are covered by multilateral procedures and negotiations.[39]

---

[39] John Jackson, 'The World Trade Organization: Watershed Innovation or Cautious Small Step Forward?', in Sven Arndt and Chris Milner (eds.), *The World Economy: Global Trade Policy 1995*, Oxford: Blackwell, 1995, p. 24. A recent set of studies relating to the agency is contained in Anne O. Krueger (ed.), *The WTO as an International Organization*, Chicago: University of Chicago Press, 1998.

Energy Policies

Fourth, energy policies became clearly less interventionist over the period. This can be seen in two contrasting declarations of policy that were adopted at different dates by the Governing Board of the International Energy Agency (IEA).[40] The earlier statement, which dates from 1977, is a thoroughly *dirigiste* document. Goals and directions of change are specified in physical terms, mostly in the context of reducing dependence on energy in general and oil in particular, with administrative measures on the part of governments as the means to realising change. The word 'markets' is not to be found in the statement; and though prices are mentioned, it is chiefly by way of stipulating that they should be consistent with the predetermined objectives. Symptomatic of the whole approach is that the list of agreed 'Principles' includes 'Concentration of the use of natural gas on premium users' requirements [*sic*]'. By contrast, the second sentence of the 1993 statement reads: 'In formulating energy policies, the establishment of free and open markets is a fundamental point of departure.' The change in tone and wording corresponds to the evolution of actual policies. As an IEA report of 1992 noted:

> 'From the mid 1980s there has been a significant reduction in detailed government intervention. Price controls have been lifted, subsidies reduced and barriers to trade in energy removed. In some countries state owned energy industries have been transferred to the private sector. The reduction in government involvement is continuing.'[41]

Taxation

Last, though perhaps less striking because the momentum of the mid-to-late 1980s has eased off, is the reform of *taxation* systems. At the end of the 1980s, after substantial reforms had been introduced in a number of countries, the results were summarised as follows in an OECD Secretariat report of the period:

---

[40] The first statement is '1977 IEA Principles for Energy Policy', and the second '1993 IEA Shared Goals'. Both are to be found, side by side, in Richard Scott, *IEA: The First 20 Years,* Vol. Two: *Major Policies and Actions,* Paris: OECD/IEA, 1995, pp. 381-87.

[41] International Energy Agency, *The Role of IEA Governments in Energy,* Paris, 1992, pp. 9-10.

'Although the tax burden has not fallen, tax reforms proposed and implemented, have meant that important progress has been made towards a more neutral, and allocatively more efficient, tax structure in many countries, reducing marginal rates of income tax and disincentives to work, harmonising post-tax yields on capital and spreading the net of indirect taxes.'[42]

A leading element in these changes has been a general reduction in the top marginal rates for personal taxation of incomes. At the same time, basic rates of corporate income tax have been brought down in many countries,while the tax treatment of different forms of physical capital has been made more uniform. There has been a general trend over the period as a whole, towards greater reliance on broad-based consumption taxes. As to particular countries, New Zealand ranks as the leading tax reformer within the group, with the UK, the USA and Canada also high on the list.[43]

So much for the main positive aspects – from a liberal viewpoint – of developments over this period. In three of the seven areas of policy, however, the advocates of reform in the core OECD countries have less to show, though in each case there have been some notable moves towards liberalisation.

Agriculture

One of the three is *agriculture*. Here useful indicators of the extent of interventionism are the 'producer subsidy equivalents' (PSEs) which are measures of support computed annually by the OECD Secretariat for both products and countries. Broadly, the past two decades fall into two sub-periods. In the first, from the late 1970s to the mid-to-late 1980s, the PSEs rose virtually everywhere. As between the three-year periods 1979-81 and 1986-88, in the largest countries or country groupings, support as a percentage of the value of agricultural production rose from 14 to 30 for the US, from 20 to 42 for Canada, from 36 to 48 for the EU, and from 60 to 73 for Japan. In 1987 came a turning point. The then OECD governments formally agreed, in the Ministerial Council Communiqué of that

---

[42] The quotation is from Chapter 5 of OECD, *Economies in Transition: Structural Adjustment in OECD Countries*, Paris, 1989, p. 209. The author of this chapter was Robert Price.

[43] The main developments are summarised in the OECD's *Economic Outlook 63*, Paris, 1998, pp. 157-70.

year, that 'a concerted reform of agricultural policies' should be implemented; and among the principles that were listed as the basis for reform the first was that 'The long-term objective is to allow market signals to influence...the orientation of agricultural production'.[44] Since then the collective wish and intention to introduce reforms have been regularly reaffirmed – most recently at the meeting of OECD agriculture ministers in March 1998 – the more so following the GATT Uruguay Round Agreement on Agriculture of 1994 and because of continuing pressures on government budgets. Some progress has been made in reducing overall support and shifting to less trade-distorting policy measures, but much remains to be done. In recent years the percentage PSE has fallen in all member countries, from an average OECD level of 45 per cent in 1986-88 to 35 per cent in 1997; but there have been only slight falls in the EU and Japan, while the milk, sugar and rice sectors appear as stubbornly resistant to attempts at fundamental reform.

Labour Markets

A central area of policy, where in many cases persisting high rates of unemployment give grounds for concern, is that of *labour markets*. Here a 1998 OECD review of developments gives a generally favourable account of the recent evolution of policies, and notes that over the 1990s estimated 'structural' (as opposed to 'cyclical') unemployment rates have moved down in several countries – Denmark, the Netherlands, Ireland, the UK, Australia and New Zealand.[45] Viewing the period as a whole, however, only two of the core OECD countries, the UK through a series of legislative reforms over the period since 1980, and New Zealand chiefly as a result of the Employment Contracts Act of 1991, appear as radical reformers. Among Continental European countries, the Netherlands alone 'pursued a comprehensive reform

---

[44] The relevant section of the 1987 Communique is quoted in OECD, *Agricultural Policies, Markets and Trade in OECD Countries: Monitoring and Evaluation 1998*, Paris, 1998, and the annual OECD *Monitoring* reports are the source of the figures given in the text. The Communiqué wording just quoted may seem innocuous, but it was agreed to only with great difficulty and marked a significant change in official attitudes and goals.

[45] OECD, *Economic Outlook 63*, pp. 171-78.

programme starting in the first half of the 1980s'.[46] Elsewhere in this group, generally speaking, prevailing and highly regulated systems have been subject only to changes at the margin. Over the years the changes have been numerous, and in many cases their effect has been to widen the scope for markets – for example, by relaxing restrictions on part-time working. But it would not be difficult to compile a list of measures or decisions which went in the opposite direction: leading examples from recent years are the harmonising of wage levels in East and West Germany following unification – an outstanding case where imposed uniformity has brought economic disintegration within a country – and the recent introduction in France of a statutory 35-hour week as from the year 2000. In Australia, a centralised system of wage determination has so far been subjected to only modest reforms. In the US, a system which is notably freer than those of other core OECD countries may on balance have become more regulated in recent years, in part through new legislation but also as a result of court rulings which have undermined the freedom of employers to terminate contracts of employment.[47]

In this context, concerns about growing over-regulation appear well-based. As Richard Epstein has written:

'Worldwide, the regulation of labor markets has created a legal edifice of stunning complexity. Protective laws abound on every conceivable aspect of the subject: health, safety, wages, pensions, unionization, hiring, promotion, dismissal, leave, retirement, discrimination, access and disability. The multiple systems of regulation now in place often work at cross purposes with each other.'[48]

It may be that for most of the core OECD countries, if one takes account of the whole range of labour market regulations including in particular anti-discrimination laws, the prevailing tendency over the period as a whole has been to move the system further away from liberal norms.[49]

---

[46] OECD, *Implementing the Jobs Strategy: Member Countries' Experience*, Paris, 1997, p.12.

[47] *Cf.* David R. Henderson (a different David Henderson!), 'The Europeanization of the U.S. Labor Market', *Public Interest*, No. 113, 1993.

[48] Richard Epstein, *Simple Rules for a Complex World*, Cambridge, MA: Harvard University Press, 1995, p. 151.

[49] Anti-discrimination laws in the US are the subject of Richard Epstein's study, *Forbidden*

Public Spending

Finally, a central issue remains that of curbing high levels of *public spending*. Some evidence on changes in the ratio of general government expenditure to GDP over the period from 1970 to 1996 is presented in Table 4, which gives data for 13 core OECD countries including all the largest economies which form the G7 group. For 11 of these countries, for which the data go back to 1970, the ratios for that year ranged from 19 per cent in the case of Japan to almost 43 per cent in the case of Sweden, with an unweighted average of just over 34 per cent. For 1996, the corresponding average was 15 percentage points higher, at over 49 per cent. The lowest ratio, which had now become that of the US rather than Japan, was close to 33 per cent, while the highest of all, for Sweden again, had risen to over 64 per cent. In terms of percentage points rounded off, the increases for individual countries, over these 26 years, range from three points for the US to 22 points for Spain. Only for two of these countries besides the US (the UK and the Netherlands) has the increase in the ratio over the whole 26-year period been held below 10 percentage points.

In looking at these longer-term changes, however, much depends on the choice of periods for comparison. This can be seen in the case of the G7 countries over the period from 1973 to 1996. In 1973, the public expenditure ratio for the group as a whole was 31.1 per cent, while for 1996 it was 39.3 per cent: hence the increase over the whole 23 years comes to 8.2 percentage points. But the opening two-year period, 1973-75, accounts for *over half* this total increase – 4.7 points, as compared with only 3.5 points for the remaining 21 years; and as between 1983 and 1996, there is only a slight increase. In the British case, the ratio actually fell as between 1975 and 1996, following an increase of 6.4 percentage points in the preceding two years.

For all 12 countries for which data for the entire period are shown in the Table, the public expenditure ratio rose in 1973-75. For all but one of these countries, Germany, there were further increases over the period 1975-83, which in some cases were substantial – for Sweden, there was a rise of 16 percentage points.

Grounds: The Case against Employment Discrimination Laws, Cambridge, MA: Harvard University Press, 1992.

Table 4: Public Expenditure Ratios, 1970-96, for 13 Core OECD Countries, Selected Years

	1970	1973	1975	1983	1989	1993	1996
US	30.0	29.1	32.8	33.4	31.9	33.8	32.7
Japan	19.0	21.9	26.8	33.3	30.6	33.7	36.2
Germany	38.3	41.1	48.4	47.8	44.8	49.5	48.8
France	38.5	38.3	43.4	51.4	49.1	55.0	54.8
Italy	33.0	36.6	41.5	48.9	51.4	57.4	52.7
UK	36.7	38.0	44.4	44.7	37.6	43.6	41.8
Canada	33.5	34.0	38.5	45.3	43.1	49.4	44.7
G7 total	30.3	31.1	35.8	38.6	36.6	40.2	39.3
Australia	..	25.5	31.4	35.0	33.0	37.3	36.4
Belgium	41.8	45.4	50.7	63.1	53.6	56.1	53.0
Ireland	..	..	..	51.9	38.7	40.8	36.6
Netherlands	41.3	43.4	50.2	59.8	53.9	55.1	49.6
Spain	21.6	22.3	24.3	37.7	40.9	47.6	43.6
Sweden	42.8	44.3	48.4	64.5	58.3	71.0	64.3

Note: Figures are for general government total outlay as a percentage of nominal GDP.
Source: OECD Secretariat.

As from the early 1980s, however, for some of the core OECD countries, the rising trend has been halted or reversed. Over the period 1983-96, three of these in particular – Ireland, Belgium and the Netherlands – show very large reductions in the ratio.[50] This is true also of the UK, where the figure was brought down substantially during the phase of rapid economic growth between 1983 and 1989. Here, however, there was an increase again over the ensuing four years, so that over the whole period 1983-96 there is only a modest fall, of 2.5 percentage points.

Until recently at any rate, these four cases were not representative of the group. In 14 other core OECD countries for which there are comparable published figures from the early 1980s, there were further increases in the ratio, which in some cases were considerable, as between 1983 and 1993. Since then, however, a change has occurred: the ratio has been brought down in all but one

---

[50] As from a later date, New Zealand also comes into this reforming category: it is omitted from Table 4 because fully comparable data are lacking.

of these 18 countries, the exception being Japan.[51] In three cases – Norway, the Netherlands and Sweden – the reduction exceeds five percentage points, while in four others – Canada, Greece, Ireland and Italy – it lies between four and five points.

The long-term tendency for the growth of public spending to outrun the growth of GDP was not long ago made the focal point of a survey article in *The Economist* by Clive Crook, in which the conclusion is drawn that – to quote the cover headline for *The Economist* that week – 'big government is still in charge'.[52] On the evidence shown here, this verdict appears broadly correct but too unqualified. It is true that, despite the various efforts made and any number of good resolutions, few of the core OECD countries have as yet achieved reductions in the ratio of public spending to GDP which are both substantial and clearly more than temporary, and that these exceptions do not as yet include any of the G7 group. On the other hand, it may yet prove, for some at least of the remaining majority, that a turning point was reached in the early 1990s, after which the growth of the public sector was effectively restrained.

Largely with a view to containing public expenditure, governments in all the core OECD countries have been trying, no doubt with varying success, to raise the effectiveness of public sector operations. This has been reflected in 'a range of management reforms including more extensive use of market-oriented approaches to resource allocation and service provision; greater managerial flexibility; and systematic rationalisation of government regulation'.[53] A notable feature has been the opening up of public procurement, and the public provision of goods and services, to competition from private businesses. For the UK, indeed – and the same might be said for New Zealand – these reforms can be viewed, in conjunction with privatisation, as having embodied an ambitious strategy to reorder the working of public

---

[51] The information in this paragraph is taken from OECD, *Economic Outlook 63*, Paris, 1998, Annex Table 28. This table shows annual series for 21 'core' OECD countries (as also for Korea), but here I have omitted Iceland on grounds of size and Denmark and New Zealand because the figures relating to them are not fully comparable with the rest. This explains the figure of 18 countries referred to here.

[52] Clive Crook, 'The Future of the State', *The Economist*, 20-26 September 1997.

[53] OECD, *Assessing Structural Reform, op. cit.*, p.10.

administration and government: this is the theme of an interesting recent study of the British case by Sir Christopher Foster and Francis Plowden.[54] However, it would not be correct, even for Britain, to identify the economic reforms of the past two decades with what these authors term 'the new public management', since this would leave out of account the extensive liberalisation that has gone ahead in other areas of policy – most notably, in relation to international transactions.

Developing Countries

In the developing world, it is in relation to external economic policies that the most striking changes have occurred: in a growing number of cases, both the policies themselves and the received ideas that bear on them have become more liberal. Here again, Chile appears as the first of the reformers, well before the close of the 1970s;[55] and in China, the process of opening the economy to foreign trade and direct investment goes back to the early days of reform. But it was later, from around the mid-1980s, that the process of external liberalisation gathered momentum among the developing countries more generally. As to actions, this was reflected in a variety of unilateral measures to liberalise trade régimes, most conspicuously in East Asia and Latin America, and to remove restrictions and prohibitions on inward direct investment.[56] As to attitudes and philosophy, there was a growing

[54] Christopher D. Foster and Francis J. Plowden, *The State under Stress*, Buckingham: Open University Press, 1996. The study raises important administrative and political issues which are not considered here.

[55] 'Between 1974 and 1979 Chile was transformed from a highly closed economy, where international transactions were severely repressed, into an open economy.'(Sebastian Edwards and Alejandra Cox Edwards, *Monetarism and Liberalization: The Chilean Experiment*, Cambridge, MA: Ballinger, 1987, p. 109.)

[56] John Dunning, in a paper published in 1995, noted that 'In the last five years alone... over eighty countries have liberalized their policies towards inward FDI'. (John H. Dunning, 'The Role of Foreign Direct Investment in a Globalizing Economy', *BNL Quarterly Review*, No. 193, June 1995.) The majority of these would be developing countries, though no doubt the list included members of the third of the groups distinguished here, the former communist countries. A recent OECD study summarises the evolution of policies towards FDI in six 'emerging economies'- Argentina, Brazil, Chile, Indonesia, Malaysia and the Philippines - all of which 'are converging on a more open approach'. (*Foreign Direct Investment and Economic Development: Lessons from Six Emerging Economies*, Paris: OECD, 1998, p. 8. The author of the study is Stephen Thomsen.)

recognition that the prosperity of developing countries did not depend on securing a range of unreciprocated favours from the rich countries, and could be increased by a general reduction in trade barriers: a striking indication of this change of heart has been the growing membership of, and a fuller participation in, what was the GATT and is now the WTO. This new orientation on the part of an increasing number of developing countries has affected the whole climate of international trade relations: it helped to make possible the launching of the Uruguay Round in 1986,[57] and it has improved the prospects for further liberalisation in the international system as a whole, both of trade and of foreign direct investment.

A second notable aspect of reform in the developing countries has been the spread of privatisation. Here the earliest substantial programme, the first of a series, was adopted in Chile during the mid-1970s. Over the past 10 to 15 years there have been major developments in Latin American countries, with Argentina, Chile and Mexico as the leading instances, and in a number of East Asian countries including South Korea and Malaysia. Even in India some first steps in this direction have been taken: an interesting case, where the initiative has come from a State government, is privatisation of electricity supply in Orissa. Admittedly, the extent to which privatisation has been taken in the group as a whole is still limited: a recent World Bank report notes that

'the state enterprise sector has diminished only in the former socialist economies and in a few middle-income countries. In most developing countries, particularly the poorest, bureaucrats run as much of the economy as ever'.[58]

All the same, a new chapter in the evolution of economic policies has been opened in a growing number of developing countries,

---

[57] John Croome, in his book *Reshaping the World Trade System: A History of the Uruguay Round* (Geneva: WTO, 1995), records that in the mid-1985 meeting of the GATT Council there was strong opposition to the idea of a new trade round from a group of 24 'hardline' developing countries. By the following spring, however, the 24 had been reduced to 10 only, and soon afterwards Argentina became another defector.

[58] World Bank, *World Development Indicators*, Washington, DC, 1997, p. 247. For the petroleum industry, Morris Adelman holds that 'most of the world's oil is still produced by flabby national dinosaurs' - though even here, there has been privatisation, as in the UK and more recently Argentina. (Morris Adelman, *The Genie out of the Bottle: World Oil since 1970*, Cambridge, MA: MIT Press, 1995, p. 8.)

including most of the larger economies among them.

It is not only through privatising state enterprises that the scope for private initiative has been enlarged. China is a notable example where

> 'There has been no formal reversion to capitalist property rights through privatisation of state property, but *de facto*, peasants have substantially regained control of their land, private house ownership is growing rapidly, and there is substantial scope for individual enrichment through private and quasi-private entrepreneurship'.[59]

In Chinese agriculture, collectivised production has virtually disappeared, and even though land is not privately owned the whole system has been opened up, in particular through long-term leasing arrangements, so as to give far more scope to markets and private initiative. In industry, recently-published Chinese official data, quoted by Maddison, show the proportion of gross industrial output contributed by state-owned enterprises in 1996 as just under 40 per cent, as compared with almost 78 per cent in 1978. In India, as part of the process of reform which was set in motion in 1991, the licensing requirement for industrial investments has been substantially removed, while the list of industries reserved for public sector enterprises has been reduced. In many countries, the scope has been widened for private businesses, often foreign-owned, to participate in investment or mineral exploration projects through joint ventures or some form of joint financing.

The Former Communist World

A third category of reforming countries emerged, as from the end of the 1980s, with the collapse of communism in Central and Eastern Europe and the former Soviet Union. In all these countries, the downfall and discrediting of the Soviet system may have opened the way to the eventual establishment of market economies. It is true that the extent of liberalisation has up to now been variable across countries and uneven within them, while in a good many cases there is as yet little to show. But for several of the group – the Czech Republic, Estonia, Hungary, Lithuania, Poland, Slovenia – the transition to a Western-type system is clearly in course of

---

[59] Maddison, *Chinese Economic Performance in the Long Run, op. cit.*, p. 61.

realisation, and in many if not most others some important steps have been taken while the general direction of change has been largely accepted. In Russia, the largest economy within the group, substantial reforms were introduced in the early 1990s: one verdict on these is that 'there can be no doubt that the reforms which began with Gaidar's price liberalisation in January 1992, and continued with Chubais's mass privatization... have led to the emergence of a genuine market economy'.[60] More recently, as events during 1998 have shown all too clearly, progress has not been well sustained, while the current economic and political crisis has put in question, among other things, the future of reform and possibly even the general direction of policy. All the same, substantial and possibly decisive changes have been made over the 1990s, while up to now the reformist orientation of official policies has not been abandoned or repudiated.

As in the other two country groupings, external liberalisation has been a leading element in the reform programmes in Central and Eastern Europe and the former Soviet Union. In a survey of the transition process, Peter Murrell has noted that

'Within just a few years, three-quarters of [these] countries abandoned centrally managed trade, removed most quantitative restrictions, reduced tariffs to fairly low levels and adopted essentially full convertibility on current account'.

More broadly, in the same article, the author concludes that 'Taken as a whole, this is the most dramatic episode of economic liberalization in economic history'.[61] The full significance of these developments does not emerge from the dry statistical indicators of Table 3 above, which give no hint that the changes in orientation thus recorded mark the end of an era. The collapse of communism has discredited a hugely influential vision of the future of

---

[60] The quotation is from Brigitte Granville, *The Success of Russian Economic Reforms*, London: Royal Institute of International Affairs (International Economics Programme), 1995, p. 105. More recently, the same broad assessment was made by Anders Aslund: 'Today, Russia has become a market economy, with dominant private ownership, though it is a rather distorted market economy.' (Anders Aslund (ed.), *Russia's Economic Transformation in the 1990s*, London: Pinter, 1997, p. 188.)

[61] Peter Murrell, 'How Far Has the Transition Progressed?', *Journal of Economic Perspectives*, Vol. 10, No. 2, Spring 1996, p. 31.

humanity, together with the prolonged and calamitous giant exercise in social engineering that was based on it.

Convergence

One of the features and results of liberalisation and its spread across the world is that the differences between economic systems and prevailing economic philosophies in the three groups of countries have become increasingly less pronounced. In all three, there have been reforms of a broadly similar kind, introduced for much the same reasons; and in particular, both privatisation and the liberalisation of cross-border transactions have become accepted and been carried into effect to a surprising extent. As to ways of thinking, there is now no serious support in the world for the idea of a fully socialist economy, and general agreement that many of the former boundaries between central direction and individual choice had to be redrawn. In both the developing countries and the former communist countries, there is now a much greater sense of belonging to the same world, the same universe of discourse, as the core OECD countries which until recently were officially viewed either as rival systems or as agents of dominance and deprivation.

This convergence in thinking and policies helps to account for the trend towards closer international economic integration which has been a notable feature of these years, and which deserves a heading of its own.

The Evolving International Economic System: 'Globalisation' and its Effects

Commentators are apt to tell us that We Stand at the Dawn of a New Era. One present-day variant of this attention-arousing message is that the world economy has been transformed in recent years by a process of 'globalisation'. According to the purest versions of this brand of DNE thinking, globalisation is a recent and dramatic development, largely independent of the wishes and intentions of governments; and it is already virtually complete, so that the world economy is now close to being a single borderless entity in which national states no longer have the power to decide economic policies for themselves. In the context of recent economic reforms and their significance, it is worth noting that all of this is misleading or false.[62]

So far from being a new development, the trend towards closer cross-border integration has been clearly in evidence over the past half-century, and can indeed be traced back at any rate to the years following the end of the Napoleonic Wars. Evidence for this can be seen in Table 5, which shows comparative annual average growth rates for world output and the volume of world exports in each of six periods spanning the years 1820-1996. In the Table there is only one time-phase, from 1913 to 1950, in which export growth fell short of output growth; and here exceptional factors were at work, in the form of two world wars and the Great Depression of the 1930s. In these six periods, the ratio of export growth to output growth, which is one indicator of the speed with which integration was going ahead, appears as highest for the half-century to 1870, while the growth rate of world exports was appreciably higher, both absolutely and relatively, in the period 1950-73 than in 1973-92 (since when it has risen again). It is not at all the case, therefore, at any rate for merchandise trade, that the past 10-15 years have brought a new and unprecedented era of globalisation.

Over these past two decades, as before, international economic integration has moved forward in response to two main interrelated factors, technical and political. Some recent technical changes, such as the further development of air freight and (still more) advances in information technology, have promoted integration by reducing the relative cost of cross-border transactions. Besides their direct impact, these have been one influence among many on external economic policies: they have made governments more favourably disposed to external liberalisation or less able to resist it. However, there is nothing new in this: the 19th century had its counterparts – most notably, perhaps, in the establishment of international cable communication. In any case, the main single factor has been, and still remains, the political one. Historically, it is national governments that have largely decided how far their economies should be open to flows of trade, capital and migrants, and this is

---

[62] A prominent 'international dawnist' author is Kenichi Ohmae, who has written a book called *The Borderless World* (New York: HarperCollins, 1990) and another called *The End of the Nation State* (London: HarperCollins, 1995). Both titles carry exaggeration to the point of fantasy.

Table 5: Growth Rates of World Output and Exports, 1820-1997 (average annual compound percentage rates of growth)

	1820-70	1870-1913	1913-50	1950-73	1973-92	1992-97
Output	1.0	2.1	1.9	4.9	3.0	3.7
Exports	4.2	3.4	1.3	7.0	4.0	8.1

Sources: For 1820-1992, Maddison, *Monitoring the World Economy*. For 1992-97, IMF *World Economic Outlook*. The final figure in the table relates to world merchandise trade rather than world exports.

still the case. Globalisation is sometimes presented as a kind of economic tidal wave, an inexorable force which is sweeping governments, businesses and peoples before it. There is an element of truth in this, but the picture is often overdrawn. Now as earlier, the story of international economic integration – and disintegration also – is predominantly one of the changing external policies of national sovereign states.

Clear evidence of this, for the years since the end of the Second World War, is to be seen in the wide differences that emerged among countries with respect to the relationship between trade growth and output growth. Within the core OECD countries, for example, Maddison's constant-price series shows for Australia in 1950 a ratio of exports to GDP of 9.1 per cent, while the corresponding figure for the Netherlands, an economy of much the same size in terms of population and GDP, was not much higher, at 12.5 per cent. By 1973 the respective ratios had become 11.2 per cent and 41.7 per cent. This striking divergence occurred chiefly because governments in the Netherlands chose to introduce substantial trade liberalisation – in the Marshall Plan agreements, as a result of EC membership, and through participation in the GATT rounds – whereas their Australian counterparts did not. Among developing countries, there is a similar conspicuous contrast, from the 1950s onward, between countries such as South Korea and Taiwan on the one hand, where the system was made more open to trade, and the more typical cases, with India as an outstanding example, where it was kept relatively closed. In every country, the character and evolution of the trade régime was largely a matter of deliberate choice.

That is still the case today. There remain wide differences in the extent to which different national economies are open to trade and capital flows. Not only these continuing differences, but also the various recent measures of trade liberalisation noted above, whether national, regional or multilateral, have reflected the wishes and decisions of the individual governments concerned.

The same is true for flows of foreign direct investment (FDI) as distinct from trade. Here growth has been more focused on the past 20 years or so, over which, though with much larger year-to-year variations, it has exceeded that of world trade. A recent estimate suggests that over the decade from 1986 to 1996 world inflows of FDI increased in real terms by a factor of more than four and one-half. By contrast, the volume of world trade over the same period approximately doubled.[63] A strong impulse to cross-border links and operations on the part of businesses has come from developments in products, markets and (especially) communications and management systems which have increased the advantages of operating globally. But here also the main causal factor has probably been changes in official policies, through privatisation and industry deregulation, which have opened up new possibilities for firms to operate across national boundaries, and by the freeing of investment flows, inward and outward, from prohibitions and restrictions.[64]Although these changes were influenced by outside events, they were not forced on the governments concerned.

Limits to Integration

One variant of DNE globalism is that the collapse of Soviet communism, either alone or in conjunction with external liberalisation on the part of developing countries, has transformed the world economy. Thus John Gray has recently argued that 'By removing from the world any alternative economic system, the Soviet debacle allowed a truly global capitalism to develop, the

---

[63] For FDI flows, the figure here is taken from the UN *World Investment Report for 1997*, which has a table (p. 269) showing year-by-year growth rates of world FDI inflows in both nominal and real terms. The figure for the growth in world trade is from IMF sources.

[64] *Cf.*, for example, successive issues of the *World Investment Report*, as also the article cited above, by John H. Dunning.

destructive consequences of which are prefigured in Marx's thought'; and on the same lines, though including the developing countries also (and with no hint as to supposed 'destructive consequences'), Jeffrey Sachs has written that

'In the last ten years, arguably in the last twenty years, a truly global market-based system has taken shape at blinding speed... a system that twenty years ago was typically portrayed as a world structure of competing systems...has suddenly become a single integrated world...'[65]

Both statements, and others of the same genre, overstate the extent to which policy reforms in these countries, as distinct from other forces at work, have in these last few years given rise to closer international economic integration. Not surprisingly, none of the newly-reforming economies has moved to a wholly liberal trade and investment régime; even had they done so, the full effects would have been less immediate than implied here; and even these full effects would be one influence only on the progress of integration, which also depends (and to a greater extent) on what happens in the core OECD countries which still account for some 60 per cent of world output and a higher proportion of both international trade and foreign direct investment. The 'Soviet debacle' was a truly historic event, but it did not in itself, and virtually overnight, create a new and fully global economic system.

Although the various measures taken to liberalise trade and capital flows over the past two decades have been far-reaching, and have extended to a much wider range of countries than at any earlier stage in the past half-century, they have by no means brought about a fully integrated world economy, nor is such a 'borderless world' even remotely in prospect. With respect to both trade and capital flows, substantial restrictions remain in place almost everywhere. For the OECD countries, the most conspicuous of these are the numerous forms of selective trade protectionism that still prevail – most notably, in agriculture, textiles and clothing, steel, automobiles, and semi-conductors; with respect to many if not most services; in government procurement practices; in the

---

[65] John Gray, 'Hollow Triumph', *The Times Literary Supplement*, 8 May 1998, and Jeffrey Sachs, 'Managing Global Capitalism', the David Finch Inaugural Lecture, University of Melbourne, 1997.

application of the complex rules of origin that have become more pervasive as a result of the spread of regional integration agreements; and through actions, and the threat of actions, under anti-dumping legislation. At the same time, as the chequered fortunes of the proposed OECD Multilateral Agreement on Investment have recently shown, many OECD governments are reluctant to remove their remaining restrictions on inward direct investment. In most developing countries, levels of protection remain higher than in the OECD group; and despite the spread of more liberal ideas and practices in recent years, the hold of 'insulationist' conceptions of both international trade relations and direct foreign investment remains strong. In every country, except where regional integration agreements apply, international migration remains strictly controlled, and in some cases, such as Australia and New Zealand, the recent tendency has been towards closer restrictions on entry.[66] None of these forms of restriction, most of them highly illiberal, is in course of being washed away by a tide of events which governments are powerless to affect.

Have Governments Lost the Power to Act?

It is often maintained today that full freedom of international capital flows, with the breakdown or abolition of exchange controls and the greater cross-border mobility of direct investment by multinational firms, now places new and much stricter limits on the freedom of action of governments. Up to a point this is true, probably increasingly so. In any case, the purpose and effect of external liberalisation, of trade as well as of capital flows, is to limit the autonomy of national governments, albeit in ways that they themselves have chosen to accept and which – as history shows – are not necessarily binding for ever. At the same time, the argument is often overdone.[67] In particular, it is misleading to suggest that power has been passing from governments to markets, and hence – as a result of their increasing prominence in these markets – to multinational firms. Generally speaking, market outcomes do not

---

[66] The issue of international migration poses some difficult problems for economic liberals, not considered here.

[67] The main issues here were well reviewed in a survey article on 'The World Economy', written by Pam Woodall and published in *The Economist*, 7 October 1995.

reflect the exercise of power – all the less so if, as a direct result of the liberalisation of trade and direct investment flows, the markets in question are made more competitive. In so far as governments relax or relinquish coercive powers, the strong probability is that the exercise of power as such has correspondingly less influence on events: it is not the case that at any given time there is a fixed quota of power in the system which has to find an outlet somewhere. As Hayek has rightly said in relation to longer-run historical evolution, within and across national frontiers, the development of a market order has in fact brought with it 'the greatest reduction of arbitrary power ever achieved'.[68]

More generally, it is a mistake to suppose either that the power to regulate international transactions effectively insulates government policies from outside influences, or that a liberal trade and payments régime prevents the exercise of effective sovereignty. Both points are well illustrated by British economic history. On the one hand, the experience of the United Kingdom right through the three decades after the Second World War demonstrates that economies where trade and payments are heavily controlled may be subject none the less to continuing external problems and crises. At the other end of the spectrum of policies, the UK during the period from 1850 to 1914 maintained virtually full freedom not only of trade and capital flows but also of migration, within an international system which was itself arguably more liberal than that of today, yet its sovereignty and freedom of action were not undermined as a result. As to today's situation, even in the highly unlikely event that an economically borderless world came to pass, the separate identity of national states, and their central political role, might well remain largely unaffected: these states, if they chose, could continue to run their own affairs in such matters as defence, foreign policy, constitutional arrangements, legal systems,

<hr />

[68] F.A. Hayek, *Law, Legislation and Liberty*, Vol. 2: *The Mirage of Social Justice*, London: Routledge & Kegan Paul, 1976, p.99. The idea that power is passing from national states to multinational firms is one of the main themes of Susan Strange's recent book, *The Retreat of the State: The Diffusion of Power in the World Economy*, Cambridge: Cambridge University Press, 1998. Her argument, however, rests on a highly questionable conception of power in which it is 'gauged by influence over outcomes' (p. 53). So broad a definition blurs the critical distinction between the exercise of coercion, whether by states or other agencies, and those influences on events which do not restrict freedom of choice.

cultural affairs, education, residence, citizenship, voting rights, and the status of the national language, as well as retaining a measure of fiscal autonomy. Meanwhile, national freedom of action with respect to economic policies, including the freedom, as now, to maintain (or even restore) a wide variety of restrictions on international trade and investment, has been reduced but by no means brought to an end by recent developments. It may be that international mobility of capital in particular will increasingly tie the hands of national governments, and even undermine the rationale for their activities,[69] but such a trend still has a long way to go.

What Is New and What Is Not

Hence much of what is currently said or assumed about 'globalisation' has to be treated with reserve or disbelief. This however is not to belittle the liberalisation that has taken place over these past 20 years, and which has given renewed and often unexpected impetus to cross-border economic integration. To argue that this recent trend towards a more integrated world economy has been neither sudden nor novel, that it mainly results from policy decisions rather than impersonal and uncontrollable forces, that it has neither deprived governments of the power to frame economic policies nor undermined the role of national states, and that despite it the world economy is still a long way from full integration, is not to dismiss it as unimportant. Not only has the liberalisation of trade and capital flows been taken further during these years than previous history would have suggested was possible, but in a large number of countries, whose economies had been largely closed and whose governments had consistently rejected the liberal conception of an international economic order, what may prove an historic change in policies has been made.

Summing Up: Developments over Twenty Years

In the assessment that Milton and Rose Friedman have made of long-term trends in the United States there is a positive and a

---

[69] This is a leading theme of Richard B. McKenzie and Dwight R. Lee, *Quicksilver Capital: How the Rapid Movement of Wealth Has Changed the World*, New York: The Free Press, 1991.

negative side. In the world of actual events, they consider that on balance the cause of economic freedom has lost ground. On the other hand, they take a more favourable view of the evolution of ideas and opinions: 'Judged by ideas, we have been on the winning side... We are in the mainstream of thought, not as we were 50 years ago, members of a derided minority'. (above, pp. 8-9).

These judgements relate to the course of change in the US over half a century, whereas my concern here is with the world as a whole in the past two decades. Because of these differences in perspective, my assessment is rather different from that of the Friedmans: it is more positive with respect to the march of events, but more equivocal when it comes to the evolution of ideas and perceptions. In this latter area, there is no doubt that liberalism has made significant gains; but as will be seen below, I think it is too soon to declare a victory. This largely explains why I view the trend to freer economic systems as uneasy rather than assured.

In the realm of events, the choice of the time interval for comparison is decisive. Even for the US, there is good reason to think that on balance the fortunes of economic liberalism have improved over these past two decades, and the evidence suggests that this is true also of the great majority of countries in the world. If we draw a line in 1998, and look back just 20 years or so but no further, the broad direction of change is evident. This is notably true with respect to privatisation and the freeing of international transactions.

Of course, there is room for argument as to the significance of these developments. One has to ask whether the shift that has occurred in the orientation of policies is likely to prove lasting – whether the concrete gains made by liberalism over this period will be consolidated, further extended, or put under threat by interventionist revivals in many if not most countries.

This central issue remains to be decided. However, the past already gives grounds for thinking that the recent trend towards enlarging the domain of economic freedom is more than transient and incidental. To judge from the freedom ratings quoted above, which are consistent with other evidence, *there are few countries if any in which, over this period, the direction of change, once explicitly set on a reforming course, has as yet been deliberately and consciously reversed.* Admittedly, this gives no guarantees for the future; and it may be that in some cases, such as Russia and Malaysia, recent interventionist moves will prove to have been the first manifestations of such a reversal. Even so, the record of the past 20 years suggests that the improvement in the fortunes of economic liberalism is more than an accident of fashion or an over-reaction to passing events.

To probe this notion further, we have to go behind the record of events, and consider what has made the improvement possible.

Part 3: Interpreting the Trend

IN RELATION TO ECONOMIC EVENTS, and not least the evolution of economic policies, issues of causation are typically complex and hard to unravel. The present case is no exception: there is no simple explanation of the trend towards more market-oriented systems. Here I outline what I see as the main interacting influences, while casting doubt on some lines of thought which appear oversimplified or misleading. In doing so, I look at implications for the future; and in this context, I consider how far the turn of events has reflected a wider acceptance of, and a more assured status for, the ideas of economic liberalism.

The Political Dimension

To start with, there is a question as to how far economic reform has been linked to particular political creeds, parties or régimes. Here the main points to be made are three.

First, as can be inferred even from Tables 1 and 3 above, and is confirmed by other evidence, reforming governments have materialised not only in every region of the world but also in widely different political guises. Both democratic and authoritarian régimes have been involved. In the former category, the core OECD countries are to be found together with a substantial and growing number of countries from the developing world and the former communist grouping. At the same time, authoritarian régimes, past and present, have also been numbered among the reformers: this can be seen, among other instances, in Indonesia under Suharto, Chile under Pinochet, China since 1978 and Ghana in the 1980s, as well as in politically freer but still heavily controlled systems such as Malaysia, Singapore and (before the recent move to democracy) the Republic of Korea.

Second, and despite this heterogeneity of reforming governments, there is clearly a strong association between political and economic freedoms. During these past two decades taken as a whole, there is probably no case to be found where under a democratic government the balance in economic policies has moved towards interventionism. On the other hand, there is probably a clear majority of non-democratic countries among the 37 non-reformers referred to in Table 1, for which an index of economic freedom can be compiled, while all the other non-reformers – Cuba, Iraq, Myanmar, Sudan and so on – have highly authoritarian régimes. This is no accident. Where political rights are assured, the more extreme forms of interference with economic freedom cannot now be maintained. While democratic institutions are neither a necessary nor a sufficient condition for liberalisation, their restoration or establishment may clear the way for it.

Third, the impetus to reform has come from both sides of the conventional political divide. There have been radical reforming governments of the left, most notably, in chronological order, in China, Mexico, New Zealand and Argentina. In core OECD countries besides New Zealand, liberalisation measures have been carried through by governments with left-wing credentials, at different times over the past 20 years – in the US, under the Democratic administrations of both Carter and Clinton, and in France, Sweden, Australia, Spain, Ireland, Greece, Portugal, Finland and the UK. As to the immediate future, the prospects for continuing reform in Britain appear better with the present Labour government than they would have been if the Conservative Party had won the election of 1997.

Such developments are neither novel nor surprising. It is not the case, as is often assumed, that in this recent reform process parties of the left have stolen their opponents' clothes.[70] Historically, liberalisation has not been preached by 'conservatives' when in opposition, nor consistently practised by them when in power. Among the core OECD countries in recent years, Australia and (still more) New Zealand offer clear examples of this: in both, the economic reforms of the 1980s were accelerated, and even made possible, because right-wing governments which were not at all liberal lost office.[71] In Britain, Margaret Thatcher's retrospective

---

[70] This view is to be found, for example, in Charles Grant's biography of Jacques Delors: 'the old "fault line" between left and right – i.e., more versus less planning for the economy – has now narrowed; by the 1990s the left had accepted much of the right's free-market philosophy.' (Charles Grant, *Delors: The House that Jacques Built*, London: Nicholas Brealey, 1994, p. 1.) In fact, 'the right' had no such distinguishing philosophy in any country.

[71] In both cases, the right-wing governments concerned – of Malcom Fraser (1975-83) in Australia, and Robert Muldoon (1975-84) in New Zealand – brought in reforms, but in

view of the Conservative government which held office from 1970-74 under the leadership of Edward Heath – of which she was herself a member – is that 'it proposed and almost implemented the most radical form of socialism ever contemplated by an elected British government'.[72] In Spain, the military dictatorship of General Franco maintained a tightly regulated economy up to the initial liberalisation measures of 1959, which were adopted only in response to a situation of crisis and accepted with great reluctance by traditionalists. In France not long ago, the prime minister of the then government of the right said in an interview: 'What is the market? It is the law of the jungle, the law of nature. And what is civilisation? It is the struggle against nature.'[73] Outside the OECD area, the former nationalist régime in South Africa was deeply hostile to free markets in both its doctrine and its practice.[74] In India today, as between the two largest political groupings, it is the party of the right, the BJP, which has taken more of an anti-reform stance in its public pronouncements on economic policy.

None of this is new, strange or incongruous. Limited government is the leading principle, not of conservatism nor of 'right-wing' political thought, but of liberalism, traditional and modern; and as Hayek has argued, in a brilliant essay appended to *The Constitution of Liberty*, there are important respects in which liberalism in this sense and conservatism are at odds. In right-wing as in left-wing parties around the world, there typically have been, and still are, strongly held and influential anti-liberal views.[75] It is within political parties, rather than between them, that the balance between liberalism and interventionism is decided; and at any given time, the influences that lead to a change in this balance are likely to be at work right across the political spectrum. This has been true

---

Australia the balance between liberalism and interventionism remained much the same over the period while the New Zealand economy became far more regulated.

[72] Margaret Thatcher, *The Downing Street Years*, London: HarperCollins, 1993, p. 7.

[73] M. Edmond Balladur, quoted in the *Financial Times* of 31 December 1993.

[74] As is shown in the enlightening essay by W.H. Hutt, entitled *The Economics of the Colour Bar*, published in 1964 by the Institute of Economic Affairs.

[75] Hayek's *The Road to Serfdom*, first published in 1944, was perceptively dedicated to 'The Socialists of All Parties'.

during these past two decades; and looking ahead, it can be expected to continue to hold good.

Hence the future of economic reform in democratic countries does not depend much, and often not at all, on the political colours worn by the parties that are in power. On the one hand, governments of the right hold out no special promise for liberalisation: the Australian Coalition government elected in 1996 has provided a clear recent example. On the other hand, and arguably more significant for the future, *the liberal cause will not necessarily suffer, and may even in some cases prosper, as and when left-wing parties come to power.*

Since liberalisation cannot be accounted for in terms of a general shift in the political centre of gravity, an explanation for the recent trend has to be sought elsewhere; this brings in wider issues of how and why economic policies change course.

Interests, Ideas and Liberal Gains

Under the spell of the brilliant closing paragraph of Keynes's *General Theory*, the economics profession is prone to think of policies as being shaped by two main influences, vested interests and the ideas of economists.[76] Clive Crook, in the article referred to above, has argued that group interests have long been and will remain a dominating adverse influence on the fortunes of economic liberalism. The Friedmans, in their Epilogue reproduced above (pp. 7-9), suggest that while liberalism has now won the battle of ideas the fruits of its victory have so far been disappointing: as Milton Friedman put it in an earlier essay, 'It is hard not to be discouraged by the miniscule changes in policy that have so far been produced by a major change in public opinion' – an outcome which he attributed in part to 'the fact that our political structures give specific interests a considerable advantage over the general interest'.[77] These respective views of the situation, which share a

---

[76] J.M. Keynes, *The General Theory of Employment, Interest and Money*, London: Macmillan, 1936, p. 386. Actually, Keynes in this famous passage refers initially to the ideas of 'economists and political philosophers', but economists have understandably preferred to focus on themselves.

[77] Milton Friedman, 'Has Liberalism Failed?', a contribution to the collection of essays in honour of Arthur Seldon which was published by the IEA in 1986 under the title of *The Unfinished Agenda*, pp. 139 and 138.

qualified pessimism as to the future and a belief that 'specific interests' are highly effective as an obstacle to reform, can be taken as a point of departure.

Interests: a Powerful but Overrated Factor

Crook focuses chiefly on the continuing growth of public expenditure in general, and state transfer payments in particular, in the core OECD countries. He sees this as the predictable result of the working of modern democratic systems, advancing what may be termed a Triple Alliance theory of the growth of government:

> 'A combination of [three] elements – self-interested politicians, self-interested bureaucrats and self-interested pressure groups – may not be the whole explanation for the remarkable expansion of government this century, but it goes a long way. What it implies is a kind of democratic failure.'

He concludes that 'The evidence to date is that democracy is indeed incompatible with economic freedom, at least in a form that the classical liberals might have recognised' – whilst adding, rightly in my view, that the prospects for economic liberalism under non-democratic forms of government are worse.[78]

If correct, this would be daunting from a liberal point of view. However, the pessimism here is overdone, because the diagnosis is at fault. It is of course true that liberalisation is often contrary to the interests of vocal and well-placed interest groups. Hence it is obvious that, for the future as in the past, the pace and extent of reform in democratic countries will be constrained by public acceptability, and that governments that wish to liberalise will have to give a lot of attention to overcoming, disarming or buying off opposition from those groups which will suffer from the measures they have in mind. It is also true that these interests may receive support from politicians and civil servants who identify with their cause partly or wholly for reasons of personal and professional advantage. But this does not at all mean that the cause of further reform is doomed or blighted; for if it were true that the dominant continuing influence on the economic policies of democratic states is and has been the combined influence of pressure groups,

---

[78] Clive Crook, 'The Future of the State', *op. cit.*, pp. 25 and 55.

politicians, and bureaucrats, all of whom are motivated only by self-interest and whose interests coincide, *the reforms of the past 20 years could never have taken place.*

This can be seen from a listing of the kinds of changes that have been made. Reforming governments have reduced or eliminated tariffs and other barriers to imports, opened up formerly closed or regulated markets to new entrants, paved the way (through privatisation and 'corporatisation') for substantial reductions in staffing by large firms, imposed new taxes, raised existing rates of taxation, reduced or eliminated tax exemptions and fiscal preferences, pared down subsidies, introduced or raised charges for public services, reduced or held down various forms of public transfers and entitlements, imposed stiffer performance tests on government agencies and their employees, resisted the growth of wages and salaries in the public sector, and curbed the powers and legal privileges of trade unions and professional associations. Aside perhaps from the removal of exchange controls, it is hard to think of any measure, in the long and varied list of economic reforms over these years, that has not conflicted with the interests and wishes of some specific, well identified and influential group. All this is inconsistent with the Triple Alliance theory. Why would 'rational' ministers and officials, concerned to advance their personal interests by dispensing well-judged favours to pressure groups, go out of their way to affront so many of these groups, and to provoke gratuitously a host of new enmities?

A possible answer might be that these ministers and officials, on the basis (as ever) of a considered and well-informed maximising exercise, decided to placate other interests than those directly affected, or to pursue their own private self-regarding agenda; but besides being inconsistent with the idea of a stable and predictable Triple Alliance, this does not square with the facts. Historically, it is not easy to identify, in any country, measures or episodes of liberalisation which can be explained in terms of willing or acquiescent governments responding to pressures from interest groups. This does not mean that such groups and coalitions of interests have little influence on events: far from it. Much (though by no means all) of the history of *interventionism* can be interpreted in this way; and even more, it serves to explain successful *opposition to reform*. But the argument does not hold in reverse: in relation to *reform itself*, a different mix of influences is typically involved. When it comes to the last two decades, I find it hard to think of instances of liberalisation, across the whole range of democratic governments which have been responsible for such changes, which can be accounted for by the combined influence of specific interests and their allies in the corridors of power.

Here as in many other cases, the notion that policies and outcomes are almost wholly determined by well defined and correctly perceived sectional interests, which is often taken as an unexamined presumption in present-day economics and political science, does not accord with the facts. In part, this is because the treatment of roles and personalities is oversimplified to the point of caricature. To portray political leaders as no more than scheming opportunist nest-featherers and vote-catchers can be useful as a corrective or a point of departure. But in relation to this recent reform process, it is clearly misleading not only for such prominent figures as Ronald Reagan, Margaret Thatcher, Turgut Özal, Jacques Delors and Roger Douglas, but also for many other politicians who were involved. In the same way, it is too naïvely dismissive to think of civil servants, whether national or international, as an undifferentiated mass of faceless, dedicated rent-seekers.

Hence it is mistaken to think that coalitions of interests largely preclude economic reform in modern democratic states, or even that liberalisation has been, or is now, contingent on their support. As to *ideas*, I think that the Friedmans are right in saying that liberalism has made large gains which may prove lasting – not only in the US, which is their chief concern, but across the world. These gains have been made on two fronts – one local, within the economics profession, and the other more inclusive.

Ideas: the Liberal Element in Economic Thinking

Locally, economic liberalism has improved its status among the economists. In my opinion, this has entailed a change of emphasis within the subject, rather than a revolution. In the world of economics, liberal ways of thinking have always been a well-identified feature, a recognised part of the intellectual scenery even for those who thought little of them or condemned them. The economic reforms of recent years have given expression to ideas

74

which are characteristic of economists, as of no other group – ideas concerning the functioning and uses of free markets. The foundations here were laid over two centuries ago, with Adam Smith and Turgot as master builders; and they were later extended and strengthened, in particular with the coming in 1870-90 of the 'marginal revolution'. This perspective on issues and events is not wholly confined to economists, while within the profession itself it is often ignored, misunderstood, dismissed as unimportant, or rejected. All the same, it is an integral part of the subject, and widely accepted as at any rate a partial guide to policy. It is a *semi-consensus*.

Contrary to some versions of history, the semi-consensus was neither forgotten nor repudiated as a result of the 'Keynesian revolution'. As to Keynes himself, Robert Skidelsky rightly says that he was 'never a collectivist in the sense... [of] someone who wanted to replace private choice by government choice', and in referring to 'his crucial role in restoring economic liberalism'.[79] Nor were his disciples and followers typically anti-liberal or *étatiste*, though some of them were. Keynesian ways of thinking were not closely linked, either in logic or in practice, with a belief in the merits of protectionism, regulation, public ownership or a continuing relative growth of state transfers. Clear evidence of this is to be found in the writings of leading Keynesians, such as James Meade, and in the memoirs and reflections of economists who, during the period from the Second World War to the early 1970s, held responsible advisory positions in government.[80]

---

[79] Robert Skidelsky, *The World after Communism, op. cit.*, p. 71. A recent instance where 'Keynesianism' is wrongly placed among 'forms of collectivism' is to be found in the over-acclaimed book by Richard Cockett, *Thinking the Unthinkable: Think-Tanks and the Economic Counter-Revolution, 1931-1983,* London: HarperCollins, 1994, p. 2. Later in the book (p. 71) Cockett makes the unfounded assertion that Keynes 'was consulted by governments and politicians of all political colours – because he was telling them things that they wanted to hear'.

[80] For the UK, the main insiders' accounts are: Robert Hall, *The Robert Hall Diaries*, edited by Alec Cairncross, London: Unwin Hyman, Vol. I, 1989, Vol. II, 1991; Donald MacDougall, *Don and Mandarin: Memoirs of an Economist*, London: John Murray, 1990; and Alec Cairncross, *The Wilson Years: A Treasury Diary, 1964-69*, London: The Historian's Press, 1997.

Contrary to another common misreading of the past, it is likewise not the case that leading economists, both in this period and earlier, paved the way for expanded state programmes because of a chronic incapacity to grasp the facts of political life. This view is to be found, among many other places, in the article by Crook, where he asserts that economists are 'the ones who cleave most naïvely' to the view 'that governments are Platonic guardians – selfless servants of the public good'.[81] It is not clear when this age of innocence is supposed to have begun. As to Keynes, his scathing portrayals of the Big Four at the Versailles Conference of 1919 are enough in themselves to demonstrate his freedom from illusions about political leaders.[82] At much the same time, in what became an established and widely used treatise on the economics of public policy, the already eminent A.C. Pigou included, in a chapter headed 'Intervention by Public Authorities', the following salutary words of caution:

> 'In any industry, where there is reason to believe that the free play of self-interest will cause an amount of resources to be invested different from the amount that is required in the best interests of the national dividend, there is a *prima facie* case for public intervention. The case, however, cannot become more than a *prima facie* one, until we have considered the qualifications, which governmental agencies may be expected to possess for intervening advantageously. It is not sufficient to contrast the imperfect adjustments of unfettered private enterprise with the best adjustments that economists in their studies can imagine. For we cannot expect that any public authority will attain, or even whole-heartedly seek, that ideal. Such authorities are liable alike to ignorance, to sectional pressure and to personal corruption by private interest.'[83]

This passage dates from 1920. One could hardly have a clearer formulation of the notion of 'government failure', which is often now presented as a path-breaking recent discovery.

It might perhaps be argued that at some later stage than this, possibly in the post-Second World War decades, mainstream

---

[81] Crook, 'The Future of the State', *op. cit.*, p. 22.

[82] First published in *The Economic Consequences of the Peace*, London: Macmillan, 1920.

[83] A.C. Pigou, *The Economics of Welfare*, London: Macmillan, first edition published in 1920. The above quotation is from pp. 331-32 of a later edition.

economics underwent a general lapse into naïveté. However, it is not hard to find cautionary words about the limitations of governments in widely used texts from this later period,[84] nor do the memoirs and recollections just referred to show signs of other-worldliness.

Liberalism Downplayed

It is not the case, therefore, that mainstream economics repudiated its liberal heritage, and promoted a continuing expansion of the role of the state, under the combined influence of Keynesian ideas and a naïve belief that politicians and bureaucrats were disinterested and selfless. What is true, however, is that, as from the 1930s, both liberal ideas and their implications for economic policies became less central, less a matter of concern, within the profession generally. This was true both in the core OECD countries and in relation to 'development economics'.

In the former case, two main factors were at work. *First*, professional attention became strongly focused on macro-economic issues and a particular (Keynesian) way of viewing them: this was a natural result of the Great Depression of the 1930s and the experience of war economies that soon followed. As a result of these developments and what were seen as their lessons, the semi-consensus, with its emphasis on prices and markets, came to be viewed, not as mistaken, but as relevant only to issues that were secondary rather than central. Demand management, often associated with incomes policies, was at the centre of the stage (with economists themselves having good claims to a share in the managerial role); and in this task, for which the responsibility necessarily lay with governments, the ideas of the semi-consensus had at most a minor place. *Second*, while there was concern over the growth of public expenditure and state regulation, high and rising rates of taxation, the increasing power of trade unions and other special interests, and the risk that these trends might endanger prosperity and economic freedom, such doubts and worries were to a large extent allayed by the amazingly good sustained performance

---

[84] For example, in Arthur Lewis's *Theory of Economic Growth*, London: Allen and Unwin, 1955, possibly the most widely read and respected treatise of its time on this topic, the statement is made (p. 83) that 'Most governments are, and always have been, corrupt and inefficient'. The text offers several later variations on this theme.

77

of the OECD economies over the years from the Second World War to the early 1970s. Hence the thoroughgoing liberalism of writers such as Friedman and Hayek, and the arguments for a consistent market-oriented approach to economic policy that were developed through institutions like the Institute of Economic Affairs in Britain, appeared as interesting but rather extreme, well out of the main current of professional thinking. As a profession, economists neither endorsed nor promoted the growth of interventionism in the OECD countries, but it was common if not typical for them to disregard or acquiesce in it.

In relation to developing countries also, in the initial post-war decades, the central issues of policy were seen, even by mainstream development economists (as distinct from Marxists, 'structuralists' and others, who of course were anti-liberal and rejected the semi-consensus), as relating to macro-economic aggregates. Here again, the role of prices and markets was typically seen as secondary or even irrelevant, while the case for strategic direction by governments was widely accepted.[85]

The Liberal Revival in Modern Economics

All this has greatly changed over the past 20 years or more. As always, there remain serious differences of opinion among economists. But the professional centre of gravity has now moved closer to liberalism, and the semi-consensus, still fully recognisable in modern dress, has been restored to its earlier central status as a guide to policy. As part of this process, the ideas of Friedman and Hayek have gained much wider recognition and acceptance – as also, in relation to the developing countries, have those of Peter (now Lord) Bauer: the main stream of thinking has changed direction, so that it now embraces them.

In this, professional thinking has become more 'universalist', in the sense that the ideas of the semi-consensus are now more widely seen as applicable to different economies across the world. There has developed what John Williamson has referred to as

'... a conviction that the process of policy reform involve[s] much the

---

[85] *Cf.* Part I of I.M.D. Little, *Economic Development, op. cit.*, and Deepak Lal's *The Poverty of 'Development Economics'*, Hobart Paperback No. 16, London: Institute of Economic Affairs, second edition, 1997.

same things – stabilization where needed, liberalization and opening up everywhere – irrespective of whether it might in the past have been classified as an industrial country, whether it had been part of the socialist bloc, or whether it had been poor in the 1950s when the world was declared divided into three'.[86]

The spread of this conviction helps to account for the development already noted, by which the differences between economic philosophies across the world have narrowed.[87]

Wider Liberal Gains

It is not only among economists that such changes have taken effect. More broadly, and going beyond academic debates, the balance of informed opinion has shifted – and indeed, without this much wider movement economic reform would not have been possible. Naturally, what has counted most has been the change in what may be termed the extended professional milieu. This goes well beyond card-carrying economists (though it includes some of them), so as to cover all those who are directly involved in the continuing debate over economic policies – most notably, though by no means only, politicians, civil servants (national and international) and central bankers. In particular, as time went on, the key central economic departments in the core OECD countries gave more attention to micro-economic issues and more consistent

---

[86] John Williamson (ed.), *The Political Economy of Policy Reform*, Washington, DC: Institute of International Economics, 1994, p. 4.

[87] Of course, it can be argued that this professional convergence has its dangers. Two recent review articles in the *Journal of Economic Literature* have criticised what their respective authors see as the disposition on the part of current mainstream pro-reform economists to offer over-generalised standard diagnoses and prescriptions. Peter Murrell ('The Transition According to Cambridge, Mass.', Vol. XXXIII, No. 1, March 1995), in the context of economic reform in the former communist countries, has written of 'an emphasis on top-down reforms designed by economists, using similar policies across countries, since market systems are [taken to be] much the same everywhere' (p. 173), and of an attitude of mind which assumes 'the irrelevance of history for designing a strategy of reform' (p. 175). Similarly, William Barber, writing about the Chicago-trained reformers in Chile under Pinochet and after ('Chile con Chicago', Vol. XXXIII, No. 4, December 1995), has argued against an approach which he sees as characterised by 'a hardcore neoclassicism' and as disregarding 'The particularities of diverse cultural, institutional and historical environments' (p. 1,948). Both authors make good points, though in my view Barber undervalues by omission the reasons for thinking that liberal ideas are of general application.

support to measures of 'structural' reform. This tendency became general in the 1980s, so that by the middle of the decade pretty well every government had come into line: as can be seen in the wording of official statements and communiques, liberalisation became an accepted recipe for change.

At the same time, though in a way that was more gradual and remains less complete, the counterpart ministers and officials in developing countries, partly under the influence of the staff of the International Monetary Fund and the World Bank, came round to much the same way of thinking. As noted by a former senior IMF official:

'...the paramount need for the combined application of macroeconomic stabilization, structural adjustment, institutional reform (and, in the 1990s, good governance) became the accepted credo not only of the Bank and the Fund but also over time of the regional banks, the aid agencies of the industrial countries, and, most importantly, of an increasing number of developing countries.'[88]

The End of Communism

The gains made by liberal ways of thought have by no means been confined to these inner circles of policy-making: advances have been made on a broader front. In a growing number of countries, the change in the intellectual climate became apparent, naturally with differences in timing and extent, from the early-to-mid 1970s onward. As from the late 1980s, however, a new element has entered in, bringing with it everywhere a powerful reinforcement to the liberal cause. All over the world, ideas about political and economic systems and their future evolution have been profoundly changed by the downfall of the Soviet model. By exposing the apparently inherent weaknesses and incapacity of state-directed economic systems, this has everywhere made liberalisation appear as more natural and more acceptable. Over a large and growing number of economies, in which it had long been taken for granted that economic systems would and should be subject to state direction to a large and probably increasing extent, a different set of working assumptions now enters into the consideration and choice of economic policies. This reflects changes in the attitudes of both

---

[88] Jacques J. Polak, *The World Bank and the IMF: A Changing Relationship*, Washington, DC: Brookings Institution, 1994, p. 8.

governments and public opinion. The whole conception of long-run historical trends, of what the future is likely to hold, has been transformed.

All this suggests a brighter future for our hero than that sketched by the Friedmans and Clive Crook. Economic liberalism now has a stronger basis in the realm of ideas and opinion – in the groves of academe, the corridors of power, and more generally – than at any stage since the end of the 1920s. At the same time, past experience, including the events of the past two decades, suggests that extensive and lasting measures of liberalisation can be carried through despite the opposition of well-placed interests. However, this is not all: there are other aspects of the situation which from a liberal standpoint are less heartening.

Liberalism's Chronic Weakness

The main point here is a simple one. Both as doctrine and programme, liberalism is subject to a chronic weakness, in that its conscious adherents are, even now, so limited in numbers and so unrepresentative of even informed opinion across the world. There are few if any countries in which there is a well-supported political party or movement which openly and consistently makes classical liberalism, in the European sense of the term, its central body of doctrine, its *raison d'être*;[89] nor is there much reason to suppose that this situation will change, since it mirrors the state of public opinion generally. *The fact is that economic liberalism as such has no solid basis of general support*. In most if not all countries, majority opinion remains hostile to the idea of what is termed 'leaving it to the market', and ready still to accept and endorse a much wider role for governments than economic liberals would wish to see. There is no sign that this situation, which historically has been the norm, is now about to change.

The reasons for this pervasive weakness have to be sought primarily in the world of ideas, perceptions and attitudes, rather than interests. It is often taken for granted today that the decisive

---

[89] Until quite recently, the Czech Republic appeared as an exception, but since the split in the party that Vaclav Klaus had led, which went with its recent fall from power, this is no longer the case. Perhaps the closest approximation in the world to a party of economic liberalism is the ACT Party in New Zealand, which was formed only in 1994. It was happy to secure just over 5 per cent of the popular vote at the general election of 1996.

battle of ideas has now been won for the liberal cause. Given the extent of recent reforms, the shift in opinion just noted – among the economists, in the extended professional milieu, and more widely – and the fact that few people believe any longer in the desirability or inevitability of state socialism, there are clearly grounds for such a view. All the same, it is mistaken: in relation to economic policies, the battle of ideas is far from over, nor is an end in sight.

The Power of Do-It-Yourself Economics

In part, this is because of the strong differences of opinion among economists.[90] But a further and underrated factor is the continuing prevalence, and influence, of intuitive economic ideas which owe little or nothing to textbooks or treatises, and which have taken shape independently of the professionals: they can justly be termed 'pre-economic'. This situation is not new, nor has it changed over these past two decades. All over the world, as each day's news bears witness, such notions and beliefs retain their power to affect the state of opinion and the design of policies. There is here a whole way of viewing economic events, relationships and objectives, which I have labelled 'do-it-yourself economics' (DIYE).[91] Two features of it are worth emphasising.

First, what is in question here is not just 'popular economic fallacies', the uninstructed beliefs of ordinary and unimportant people. These same ideas are held with equal conviction, and expressed in much the same language, by political leaders, top civil servants, chief executives of businesses, general secretaries of trade unions, well-known journalists and commentators, religious leaders, senior judges and eminent professors – as also by economists themselves, in uninstructed or unguarded moments. That is why they should be taken seriously. This is not 'pop economics', since it is embraced by leaders as well as led; it is not 'voodoo economics', since those who practice it are not just cranks

---

[90] It is in my opinion going too far to suggest, as John Williamson has done, that the case for reform reflects 'the common core of wisdom embraced by all serious economists' (*The Political Economy of Policy Reform, op. cit.*, p. 18).

[91] David Henderson, *Innocence and Design: The Influence of Economic Ideas on Policy*, Oxford: Blackwell, 1986. I have also drawn here on an article of mine, 'The Revival of Economic Liberalism: Australia in an International Perspective', published in *The Australian Economic Review*, 1st Quarter 1995.

or unbalanced enthusiasts; and it is not 'businessmen's economics', since its adherents are equally to be found in many other walks of life.[92]

Second, as compared with the economists' semi-consensus, DIYE is strongly interventionist. It holds for example that products, industries and activities can be characterised as 'essential' and 'non-essential', or ranked in order of priority, independently of willingness to pay at the margin; that national self-sufficiency in essentials is a key objective, which governments are responsible for achieving; that when transactions take place across national boundaries, the state is necessarily involved, so that international economic competition is predominantly between states; that exports represent a gain to each country, and imports a loss; that bilateral trade balances between countries are rightly matters of concern and official action; that tariffs, import restrictions and export subsidies serve to increase total employment; that administrative actions to reduce or constrain the size of the labour force – such as compulsory reductions in working hours, enforced early retirement, or tighter restrictions on immigration – are bound to ease the problem of unemployment; that actions undertaken for profit, or more broadly from self-interest, are open to question as such; that when markets appear not to function well, the remedy lies with direct regulation; that market processes are often, if not inherently, chaotic, disruptive and unjust; and that the responsibility for ensuring just and effective outcomes, over a vast range of particular cases, rests with governments. All this makes for an indefinitely large regulatory agenda.

These twin features of DIYE – its high-level patronage, and its bias towards interventionism – can be seen in a host of instances, past and present. Historically, a remarkable case, or set of cases, is that explored in Hayek's fine study of the 'illegitimate extension to the phenomena of society of scientistic methods of thought', as in the collectivist teachings of Saint-Simon, Comte and their

---

[92] Here I have a friendly disagreement with Sir Samuel Brittan, who argues against the term 'do-it-yourself economics' on the grounds, which I agree with, that almost any foolish notion may win support from sophisticated economists. However, the label 'businessmen's economics', which he prefers, is misleading.

successors in both the 19th and 20th centuries.[93] A current specific example is to be found in a widely-accepted economic argument for closer European union. The main point here, a familiar one, is to be found in a speech made by Garret FitzGerald in mid-1984, when he was Prime Minister of the Republic of Ireland. He argued that there were two economic superpowers, the US and Japan, and that

> 'attempts to compete on an equal basis in the economic sphere with these super-powers by independent, individual action, are quite simply bound to fail'.

From this widely accepted premise the conclusion has been drawn, in Brussels and elsewhere, that Community-wide officially-sponsored action programmes hold the key to better economic performance in Europe and indeed to its continuing independent status. Here, for instance, is a former British Commissioner for regional policy, Bruce Millan, on policies for industry:

> 'If Europe does not develop an industrial policy, it will be invaded by Japan, the Far East, and other parts of the world.'

For research and development, a similar message came from Jacques Delors, during his time as President of the European Commission:

> 'Europe will never be built if we all continue, in piecemeal fashion, to conduct the research which is the basis for our prosperity and our hope for the future.'

On a later occasion, Delors reproached member governments for

> '... the European Council's refusal to give the Community the means, in the shape of concerted research and training projects, to encourage European companies to cooperate to become more competitive in a world dominated by economic war [sic]'.[94]

---

[93] F.A. Hayek, *The Counter-Revolution of Science: Studies on the Abuse of Reason*, Glencoe, IL: The Free Press, 1952, p. 107.

[94] FitzGerald was speaking at a conference in Brussels. The quotation from Millan is from remarks he made to a Committee of the European Parliament in the summer of 1993. The statements by Delors are from two of his annual addresses to the European Parliament: the first dates from 1985, the second from 1993.

All this makes sad reading, the more so in that both FitzGerald and Delors are economists (though both might be challenged on the credentialist grounds of today). Contrary to FitzGerald, and many others, it is not the case that competition in world markets is between states: unless governments go out of their way to engage in cross-border transactions, competition in international markets, just as within national boundaries, is between enterprises and the goods and services that these enterprises produce. Governments can influence the terms on which particular forms or products compete, for example through tariffs or subsidies or anti-dumping actions, but this does not turn them into direct front-line competitors. FitzGerald's assumption is a prime specimen of the aspect of DIYE which I have termed 'unreflecting centralism'.[95] It is likewise not the case – except in a world quite unlike our own, of closely restricted international trade – that enterprises will necessarily gain from being located in large rather than small states, as is clear from the instances of Switzerland and Hong Kong: the whole notion of an 'economic superpower' makes little sense in an open international economy. Again, it is not the case that R & D activities in European countries, or elsewhere, are primarily carried out by states as such, nor that they would necessarily be more effective if they were 'concerted' at national or at European Community level to follow what is sometimes alleged, or just assumed, to be successful American and Japanese practice. Finally, the notion that today's world is 'dominated by economic war' is not only absurd but, coming from a man in Delors's then position, deeply irresponsible. Nonetheless, these views of the world, and of the European situation, have been and continue to be highly influential.

Here as in many other cases, the eminent persons who have come to hold such opinions are far from being merely the servants of interest groups. The connection is more the other way round: such groups have been formed to exploit the opportunities opened

---

[95] Alas, it is not only those economists that have moved into politics who may lapse into unreflecting centralism of this kind. In a recent issue of the OECD's *Economic Outlook* (No. 62, dated December 1997) the statement is made (p. 40) that 'a steadily increasing number of countries now have the capacity to become active players [*sic*] in the world economy'. Cross-border transactions do not make up a game, or a drama, in which states are the participants.

up by policy decisions based on economic ideas which have carried weight in themselves. No doubt some of their appeal to political leaders derives from the fact that they assign to such individuals a prominent and innovative role: there is an element of interest here. All the same, these ideas represent genuine convictions, and indeed they are widely held by people outside political life to whom this personal motive does not at all apply.

Thus pre-economic ideas may well influence outcomes and policies, even in their own right. Viewing recent history, even in the OECD countries, a striking aspect has been the adoption, often as it would seem almost heedlessly, of far-reaching interventionist principles, measures and programmes that were based on dubious and largely unexamined economic assumptions. Two areas of policy where this is especially noticeable are energy (for example, Project Independence and the later 1978 programme in the US, the Canadian National Energy Program of 1980, and early British notions as to depletion policies for North Sea oil and gas which were based on the naïve idea that the object should be to ensure the longest possible period of national self-sufficiency), and labour markets (for instance, the growth and spread of anti-discrimination laws, the introduction of statutory provisions for earlier retirement and limitations on hours of work, and the imposition of wage uniformity). Pressure groups have been involved in some of these developments, but by no means all; and in every case DIYE has played its part.

Economists typically ignore or underestimate this factor, for two related reasons. *First*, they find it hard to believe that 'rational' agents – intelligent, highly educated, well informed, experienced and influential people, including many if not most of those in high places – are apt to view economic systems and issues in ways that are quite different from theirs. Hence they disregard the ample evidence that this is so. *Second*, as noted above, they prefer to model human behaviour in terms of well-defined and clearly articulated private interests, and therefore view the actions of politicians and officials too exclusively through the prism of public choice theory. The result, as I think, is that the profession now has a conception of history which is too circumscribed, too stylised, to place events in a true perspective.

In particular, this view of the system takes too little account of *the combined influence* of DIYE and the lobbies. Interest groups are successful not just through expert lobbying and persuasion directed towards rationally compliant politicians and bureaucrats, but also by appealing to a wider public opinion, made up of people who do not see themselves as standing to gain or lose from the way in which the issue is decided. It is when these groups can draw support from widely accepted ideas and beliefs – including especially economic ideas, not necessarily those of the professionals, relating to fairness or national interest – that their campaigns are most likely to achieve results. This is not sufficiently allowed for in the theory of public choice, which divides the population into (1) well-informed specific interests, and (2) voters who are 'rationally ignorant', and hence uninformed and inactive, in relation to questions where their immediate material interests are not at stake. But of course, people are not necessarily indifferent about issues which do not directly involve them, and which they have neither time nor inclination to investigate in full. Typical voters have ideas and opinions as to what is fair, right, just, reasonable and acceptable, and on what actions are likely to promote social or national goals of which they approve. What they think matters. Political outcomes are not necessarily decided by the politicians, officials and lobbyists alone.

Hence it is in conjunction with interest groups, rather than independently of them, that the main impact of DIYE on economic policies is often made. In such cases, though exceptions can be found, both the interests and the ideas are typically opposed to liberalisation. Now as ever, the prospects for further reform are under threat from the combination, in informal alliance, of strongly held anti-liberal economic ideas and interests which see themselves as threatened by what is proposed. This helps to account for the general absence of solid public support for liberalisation, which in turn explains why the trend to economic liberalism has been, and will probably continue to be, uneasy and unassured.

Two further points are worth making on perceptions and ideas, and both of them add weight to the pessimistic prognosis. *First*, as Crook notes in his survey article (p. 56), there is now an impression 'in many western nations' – and, I would add, in other countries also – that 'the market reforms of [recent] years went too far, and that it is time to reaffirm the role of the state'. Such a mood, even if it does not lead to a reversal of what has been done, may well constrain what is possible in this next stage.

New Forms of Anti-Liberalism

Second, I believe that anti-liberal ideas and causes have gained increasing support in recent years from three interrelated developments. The first is the rise and growing influence of environmentalism in forms which involve condemnation of or disregard for market processes and a bias towards collectivist ways of thinking and regulatory programmes. One aspect of this is opposition to greater freedom of international trade and capital flows.[96] The second is what the Friedmans, echoing Tocqueville, refer to as 'an excessive drive to equality'. This shows itself, in particular, in

- labour market legislation – in the ever-widening scope of anti-discrimination laws and through various forms of affirmative action in relation to hiring and conditions of employment, and
- affirmative action programmes in such areas as housing, the availability of credit, and admission to universities.[97]

The anti-liberal ideas which bear on these issues have increasingly found institutional expression and support – through single-interest pressure groups, in specialised areas of national administrations, and in UN agencies and international committees of experts. Part of this process has been an ever-extended interpretation of human rights in which the whole notion has become devalued and

---

[96] As for example in Tim Lang and Colin Hines, *The New Protectionism: Protecting the Future against Free Trade*, New York: New Press, 1993.

[97] An outstanding source here is the work of Thomas Sowell: two of many pertinent references are his book, *Preferential Policies: An International Perspective* (New York: William Morrow, 1990) and his Trotter Lecture, *The Quest for Cosmic Justice* (Wellington, New Zealand Business Roundtable, 1996). Going outside economics, I would mention particularly Aaron Wildavsky's *The Rise of Radical Egalitarianism* (Washington, DC: American University Press, 1991).

debased.[98]

A third related development is the growth and spread, largely within universities, of the subjects that can be grouped together under the heading of 'cultural studies' and the ways of thinking that typically go with them. Economists have given little attention to this trend, probably because their own subject has so far largely escaped the ravages of 'deconstruction', 'post-modernism' and related tendencies, while these movements in turn have not developed a systematic economic orientation or philosophy of their own which has claims to be taken seriously. But despite a lack of knowledge of, or interest in, what economists and economic historians have to say, many of the authors concerned share an aversion from, or even hatred of, what they conceive to be the essential features of capitalism in general and present-day 'global capitalism' in particular. As a recent survey of the field by two well-known academic authors expresses it:

> '...the post-modern turn is intimately bound up with globalism and the vicissitudes of transnational capitalism... In a global market capitalism, commodity markets are opening with great fanfare in China and Russia as capitalism exports its markets, products, McCulture and status consciousness round the globe, bringing with the new goodies its seamy side in the form of crime (both organized and street thug), drugs, social decay, and pathological acquisitive individualism... it appears that Marx's nightmare of a totally commodified society is becoming a reality.'[99]

Both post-modernism in its different guises and the more recent forms of egalitarianism characteristically share a vision of the world in which past history and present-day market-based economic systems are viewed in terms of patterns of oppression

---

[98] Hayek has commented on this latter aspect in Volume Two of *Law, Legislation and Liberty*, pp. 101-06.

[99] Steven Best and Douglas Kellner, *The Postmodern Turn*, New York and Brighton: Guilford Press, 1997, pp. 110 and 157. This book describes itself on the back cover as 'a groundbreaking analysis of the emergence of the postmodern paradigm'. Despite the confident assertions that are made in it about economic systems and events, the list of references, which extends to perhaps 500 books and articles, includes only a small unrepresentative handful of items which relate to economics or economic history. On the other side of the polemical divide, a well-argued critique of the impact of 'cultural studies' on historical writing is to be found in Keith Windschuttle's disturbing book, *The Killing of History*, Sydney: Macleay, 1995.

and abuses of power. Free markets and capitalism are seen as embodying and furthering male dominance, class oppression, racial intolerance, imperialist coercion and colonialist exploitation. The appeal of this profoundly anti-liberal way of thinking seems to have been little affected by the collapse of communism.

All these are grounds for pessimism about the prospects for economic liberalism. Yet the phenomena described above are for the most part not new: as noted, the weakness is chronic rather than acute. Hence the issue of causation arises here as well. If economic liberalism had and has such limited support, what is it that made possible the reforms of recent years, and is it to be expected that influences of much the same kind will operate in the future?

Accounting for Liberalisation

What is in question here, and has to be explained, is *a particular change in direction* within economic policies, the shift (on balance) from interventionism towards more liberal systems. For this, it is necessary to go beyond the conventional framework of interests and economic ideas.

As to interests, pressure groups have generally speaking not played a significant role, since liberalisation either did not figure on their agenda or was seen as contrary to their interests. There are exceptions here, perhaps most notably in relation to the abolition of exchange controls and the freeing of financial markets. But in most areas of policy, either business or labour interests, or both, were opposed to liberalisation. At the same time, both labour interests and other pressure groups have argued for tighter regulation relating to occupational health and safety, workplace practices, and the environment, and for more comprehensive anti-discrimination laws. In this, they have usually been trying, in a number of areas and countries with some success, to make economic systems *less* liberal.

As to ideas, the main positive factor – at any rate until the collapse of communism at the end of the 1980s, by which time reform was well under way in a wide range of countries – was the gradual increase in support for the economists' semi-consensus. But this did not mean that the profession became united in support of economic reform: in every reforming country, in varying degrees, dissenting economists have been well represented among the numerous critics of liberalisation. Further, even a greater measure of professional agreement would by itself have done little to launch or sustain the reforming process in any country, given the continuing prevalence of anti-liberal pre-economic ideas, the widespread opposition of interest groups, and the chronic lack of general support for economic liberalism as such. In any case, the change in professional thinking has itself to be explained.

Hence a search for causes has to go wider. In particular, allowance has to be made for the influence of events. I believe that the trend towards liberalisation can be largely attributed to *the combined impact of events and ideas on the prevailing climate of opinion*. Of the several interacting causal relationships involved, this is the one that typically bears most weight.

The Importance of Attitudes

To speak of this relationship takes us beyond the realm of economic ideas. These ideas themselves affect the general climate of opinion both within and across countries; and indeed, one can speak of a climate of opinion – a micro-climate, so to speak – within the economics profession itself. But ideas and 'climate' are not at all the same. In relation to the latter, what is in question is not formal systems of thought or well constructed arguments, but broad perceptions – views of the world, working assumptions, *attitudes*. The distinction between the two, and the extent to which outcomes are affected by attitudes, have been well brought out by Henry Phelps Brown:

> 'Attitudes do not consist of beliefs in the sense of conscious convictions or creeds: they are rather the "feeling or opinion", the presuppositions that guide our actions because they frame and focus our view of situations, and cast both ourselves and other people in roles that we take to be inherent...Because attitudes govern responses, they are among the basic determinants of the course of history.'[100]

Attitudes can thus be viewed as the medium through which policies and lines of action are constantly reassessed and reshaped. It is here that we have to look for the more immediate explanation of the recent shift in the balance between liberalism and interventionism.

---

[100] E. H. Phelps Brown, *The Origins of Trade Union Power*, Oxford: Clarendon Press, 1983, pp. 299-300.

In causing attitudes to change, it is the influence of events – of new developments, and the constructions placed on them – that has often been the main determining factor, particularly when those events were unforeseen and posed problems.

The Impact of Events

This is to be seen in actual recent episodes of reform. In many if not most of the reforming countries, the main single impulse to change has been reactive, rather than (or as well as) affirmative: reforms have resulted, not so much from an endorsement of liberal principles as such, but rather from perceptions of failure, malfunctioning or ineffectiveness within the system, perceptions which themselves arose from events and what were seen as the lessons to be drawn from them. Reforming measures have been precipitated, or made possible, by a loss of confidence – within official circles, across a wider public opinion, or both – in the policies of the past, and governments have taken the path of reform in response to what they saw as problem situations.

The problems in question have variously been acute, chronic, or a combination of the two. In the extreme case of the communist countries of Central and Eastern Europe and the former Soviet Union, the whole system was abruptly revealed as no longer viable: it was evident that a new start had to be made. In a number of other instances, the possibility for reform was likewise opened up by crises, usually external, to which a response had to be made by the government concerned, and which prompted questions about the underlying character of the policy régime and the role of the state. In different ways and in varying degrees, this applies within the core OECD countries to Turkey in 1979 and 1980, France in 1982-83, Australia at the end of 1983 and in mid-1986, New Zealand (a conspicuous case) in mid-1984, and Sweden in the early 1980s and again a decade or so later. Elsewhere much the same phenomenon can be seen in Chile after the overthrow of the Allende régime, Mexico following the debt crisis of 1982, Ghana in the early 1980s, Argentina in the late 1980s, India in 1991, and a number of East Asian countries, including most notably Indonesia and South Korea, following the successive financial crises of 1998.

A second source of pressure, sometimes linked to foreign exchange crises but often constituting a problem in its own right, has been the need to control fiscal deficits and the growth of public debt: there are numerous examples here, both in the core OECD area and more generally, where governments have found themselves forced into some combination of retrenchment and tax increases.

At the other end of the spectrum, where the element of crisis was less involved, the ground was prepared for reforming governments by chronic and growing concerns over what was seen as poor economic performance. This seems to fit the case of China. In the UK, two factors were, first, the 'inflationary explosion' of 1975, which 'led to a destruction of confidence in the general character of the economic strategies hitherto followed by successive governments',[101] and second, an increasing resentment of the behaviour, and hence of what appeared as the excessive power, of trade unions. Chronic concerns were also dominant in the US, and they go far to explain the decision by the governments of the European Community to launch and carry through the Single Market programme from the mid-1980s onwards. In several cases, such as Chile, Turkey, Mexico, New Zealand and Argentina, both the chronic and acute elements were present and mutually reinforcing. The crises gave rise to radical reform programmes (in the Turkish instance, only partly realised in the event), the case for which had already been argued independently of them.

Now there is no law which asserts that foreign exchange or fiscal crises, or general dissatisfaction with economic performance, or even both together, will necessarily lead to liberalisation. Historically, they have sometimes had the opposite result, with governments resorting more to regulation and control: this was, at least so far as initial reactions went, a common pattern during the period just after 1973. With a few exceptions, such as Chile in 1981, New Zealand in 1982, and Malaysia in 1998, this has not happened in these past 20 years (and in both the first two cases, the interventionist measures then taken were seen as, and proved to be, no more than temporary). In responding to pressures and

---

[101] Lord Croham, 'The IEA as seen from the Civil Service', in Arthur Seldon (ed.), *The Emerging Consensus*, London: Institute of Economic Affairs, 1981. Croham, a former top civil servant, notes that, while the first outcome of the loss of confidence was a rethinking of macro-economic policies, this was soon extended to a 'willingness to examine alternative ideas on all fronts'.

challenges, governments in these past two decades have typically moved in the opposite direction.[102] Here a number of mutually reinforcing factors have been at work.

Why Events Brought Liberalisation

In some areas, technical changes have either made regulations harder to enforce (financial markets being the main example) or made possible an extension of the sphere of markets and competition (as in telecommunications and electric power). Again, considerations of national competitiveness have been a factor in some cases: in financial markets especially, some governments, often with the support of the interest groups involved, have deregulated in order to keep their own national financial centres competitive with others, and a similar concern has operated against restrictions on direct foreign investment, both inward and outward. In cross-border liberalisation generally, governments have found it easier to go forward because others were doing so, within regional or multilateral agreements. In privatisation especially, there has been an international learning process which has spread to a growing number of countries.

Perhaps the most important single aspect has been the movement of ideas and attitudes both within the economics profession and more broadly – the growing belief that economic performance had suffered as a result of the increase in regulation, the malfunctioning of public enterprises, the rise in public expenditures and taxation rates, the failure to curb inflation or to bring down fiscal deficits, and the growth of trade union power. Here again, however, events had a leading if not dominant part in changing the thinking of economists as well as others. It was not logic and debating skills, but actual and disconcerting developments within economic systems, which undermined the accepted Keynesian framework of thinking in the core OECD countries, put increasingly in question the *dirigiste* approach to developing economies, and destroyed the credibility of communism, and which in doing so raised the status

---

[102] This puts in question the view expressed by Robert Higgs in his account of the growth of government in the US, that 'under modern ideological conditions almost any kind of crisis promotes expanded governmental activity...' (Robert Higgs, *Crisis and Leviathan: Critical Episodes in the Growth of American Government*, New York: Oxford University Press, 1987, p. 250.)

of the liberal semi-consensus. In economics, as with other disciplines whose subject-matter is drawn from past and current historical events, the famous aphorism of Hegel still applies: the owl of Minerva takes her flight only with the gathering of the dusk.[103]

Under these various interrelated influences, attitudes were reshaped. Both newly elected governments, which had typically come into office as a result of dissatisfaction with their predecessors, and established governments that found themselves forced to deal with awkward situations or crises, found it natural, and sometimes unavoidable, to turn to liberal measures – and often, in consequence, to liberal advisers. In some cases, as in Britain in 1979, this had in any case been an announced intention before coming into office. In a number of other countries the element of improvisation was greater; and in a few, such as France in 1982-84, earlier policies and working assumptions were jettisoned.

Two features of the process further help to explain why reforms went ahead despite the lack of support for economic liberalism as such.

First, as in many past episodes, it was not only the professed liberals who backed specific reforms. Among leading politicians, a good instance is Jacques Delors. He was a prominent reformer over a decade or more, in his successive roles as Minister of Finance in France, where he was mainly responsible for carrying through the redirection of policies just referred to, and as President of the European Commission where he was a leading architect of the Single Market; yet he has always been a staunch critic of liberal ideas in general. His support was given to particular forms of liberalisation, but in the service of wider objectives which he did not formulate in liberal terms. In other and perhaps more typical cases, politicians and civil servants who held no strong position, and in any case were mostly not economists, were affected along with others by events and trends of thinking: attitudes changed, and old assumptions about how things worked, and what was practical

---

[103] It should be added, however, that an early owl had already taken off in Chicago: the main deciding events in the OECD countries, and in particular the emergence of high rates of inflation and of unemployment as simultaneous and persistent features of these economies, had been foreseen and accounted for by Milton Friedman.

politics, were discarded. In the business community, support for cross-border liberalisation came from people who had no strong attachment to free trade or liberal ideas, but had come to think in terms of a future which would almost inevitably bring greater internationalisation and growing overseas opportunities: both interests and attitudes were involved in this. Here and elsewhere, reforms gained widespread support from influential fellow-travellers, as well as from the minority of committed liberals which itself had grown in numbers and gained some useful ground.

Second, governments were not simply the prisoners of events, nor were they purely reactive. In relation to the freeing of trade and investment flows, as noted above, they were not just carried along by a wave of 'globalisation' which they were unable to control or resist: they took far-reaching measures of their own. Again, in many countries, liberals in office, especially in newly-elected governments, were able to grasp and exploit the initiative which events had placed in their hands. As a result, liberalisation was taken well beyond what the mere response to immediate problems or crises would have suggested, sometimes in ways that had not been the subject of prior consensus: governments, or individual ministers within them, took the opportunity to launch or take forward measures and programmes which they favoured in any case. In this, while they naturally had regard to public opinion in considering when and how to liberalise, they also anticipated and tried to mould it. A good example is the privatisation programme in Britain. Here Nigel Lawson has made the point that

> 'In advance of every significant privatisation, public opinion was invariably hostile to the idea, and there was no way it could be won round except by the Government going ahead and doing it.'[104]

In such initiatives, as in the reform process as a whole, outcomes in a good many countries have been strongly influenced by the personal commitment of political leaders.

Generalising, it can be said that over this period events helped to form new attitudes, and favoured the cause of reform, in three main interrelated ways. *First*, they forced governments to react to situations and problems, usually though not always external, which

[104] Nigel Lawson, *The View from No. 11*, London: Bantam Press, 1992, p.201.

had got out of hand. *Second*, they provided new and unchallengeable evidence, most notably in the collapse of communism but also through other developments, that highly regulated economic systems function badly. *Third*, in many non-communist countries, and in China also, they provoked reflection and debate on the reasons for unsatisfactory or worsening economic performance; and in many of these countries, both among economists and in the extended professional milieu, the result was to breathe new life into the liberal semi-consensus.

Summing Up: Implications for the Future

From a liberal viewpoint, this interpretation of events has both positive and negative implications. On the positive side, the power of anti-reformist interest groups, private and public, appears as more limited than it is often said to be, while liberal ideas have both profited from the collapse of communism and made some useful gains in their own right. But despite its now more assured status in the world, economic liberalism still suffers from a lack of broad support, while anti-liberal beliefs of various kinds, some of them new, are widely held and influential. Hence the future of economic reform may well continue to depend in large part on the stimulus arising from events and the responses evoked by them; and there is no guarantee that recent history will be repeated, with events serving both to reinforce the professional semi-consensus and to push governments along a path of reform or give them, in some cases, a welcome opportunity to follow it. I turn now to look at some future possibilities more directly.

Part 4: Will the Trend to Economic Liberalism Continue?

NOW AS EVER, PREDICTING THE COURSE OF CHANGE in economic systems and policies is a high-risk undertaking: the process just described brought many surprises with it, while the current world financial turmoil, which came as a shock to the most experienced observers, has re-emphasised the limitations of economic understanding and the fragility of even short-term projections. All the same, some indications for the future of economic liberalism can be gleaned from past trends, some current developments, and what appear to be established underlying factors.

Consolidation, Momentum and Spread

To start with, I believe that, broadly speaking, and despite some recent indications to the contrary, the main reforms of these past two decades have come to stay. In particular, few governments, in any part of the world, are likely to to take back into would-be permanent public ownership industries or enterprises that have been privatised; to bring back either general price controls or the tight industry regulations and entry restrictions of the past; to restore comprehensive exchange controls (at any rate as anything other than a temporary expedient); to reintroduce prohibitions, or drastically tighten restrictions once again, on flows of direct foreign investment; or, in the end, to repudiate in any substantial way the main commitments that they have made with respect to freeing cross-border trade flows. This is not because they now have no effective choice in the matter – as was seen above, 'globalisation' has not deprived national states of freedom to decide their own policy régimes – but because perceptions, and assessments of national interests, have changed. In this respect the world has moved on. Indeed, there are areas of policy, especially those just referred to, in which the ranks of the reformers may well be gradually reinforced as time goes by, with previously non-reforming countries responding to the pressure of events, the movement of ideas, and the influence of example. There is likely to be a further momentum of liberalisation here, though just how much remains to be seen. For reasons already noted, any such momentum is unlikely to be checked significantly by the coming to power of left-of-centre governments, as most recently in Germany and Italy.

Again, if one looks at individual countries, there are indications, or clear possibilities, of a still continuing reform momentum, provided that serious political instability does not develop. In particular, this applies in cases where liberalisation is still in the early stages but some important corners, even though by no means all, seem to have been turned for good: China, India, Brazil and – even now – Russia are the outstanding examples. There is a good chance that, as in recent years, there will be a tendency across frontiers towards convergence in policy régimes, with the main steps towards convergence being taken, albeit often erratically, in a reformist direction, in the economies that are more heavily controlled.

Admittedly, all this applies mainly to those countries where political parties are free to compete for support and office, and there are accepted procedures by which changes of governments can take place without resort to force. Where authoritarian systems persist, the range of possible outcomes is greater and the prospects for economic reform are generally, though not always, worse. To take the more extreme cases, there is no clear prospect of economic reform in such countries as Cuba or Myanmar, while the coming to power of a Taliban or an Ayatollah Khomeini can bring with it, at least for a while, a wholesale onslaught on liberal ideas and freedoms of all kinds. However, as noted already, some authoritarian régimes have taken the path of reform, and the influences which have been at work in these instances may well prevail in others. In any case, the number of countries that can reasonably be called democratic has been growing in recent decades, and this trend seems likely to be maintained. Because of its broadly positive implications for economic as well as political freedom, this can be viewed as a further source of momentum.

Generally speaking, therefore, it is reasonable to expect consolidation of the main reforms have now taken hold in most if not all the leading economies of the world, along with many others, together with a gradual though uneven further spread of much the same reforms elsewhere. To this extent the prospects for economic liberalism appear favourable. However, this is not the full picture. Both immediate concerns and longer-established factors may work in the other direction.

The Impact and Lessons of Recent Crises

As from mid-1997, a new set of unforeseen and disconcerting events has extended the debate on economic reform. The crises in a number of East Asian countries, together with more recent episodes of instability in financial and foreign exchange markets, have raised in an acute form some related issues of liberalisation versus control, including in particular the question of whether international capital flows should now be made subject to closer official regulation. Broadly, two distinct morals have been drawn from these events, and though these are not incompatible they point in different directions. They rest on different interpretations of the East Asian crises.[105]

The first interpretation can be labelled 'externalist', since it views the crises as being primarily due to outside influences, rather than to weaknesses in the system or misguided economic policies within the countries affected. A good illustration is to be found in an article by Steven Radelet and Jeffrey Sachs:

> 'The crisis is a testament to the shortcomings of international capital markets and their vulnerability to sudden reversals of market confidence... The search for deeper explanations that attribute the entire massive contraction to the inevitable consequences of deep flaws in the Asian economies – such as Asian crony capitalism – seems to us mistaken.'[106]

On such a view, the liberalisation of capital account transactions was a leading contributory factor in the crises, and this establishes a *prima facie* case against allowing the unrestricted transfer at any rate of short-term international flows of funds. One leading economist with impeccable free trade credentials who has taken

---

[105] The argument here draws on a paper of mine entitled 'Industrial Policies Revisited: Lessons Old and New from East Asia and Elsewhere', issued in *Pelham Papers No. 3*, published by the Centre for the Practice of International Trade at the Melbourne Business School, 1998.

[106] Steven Radelet and Jeffrey Sachs, 'The Onset of the East Asian Crisis', paper prepared for the Brookings Institution, 1997.

this line is Jagdish Bhagwati. He argues that 'the Asian crisis cannot be separated from the excessive borrowings of short-term capital as Asian economies loosened up their capital account controls and enabled their banks and firms to borrow abroad'; that the gains from full freedom for capital flows are often overstated, and in any case have to be set against the high costs arising from 'the crises that unregulated capital flows inherently generate'; and that the pressure to abolish restrictions on all capital flows, in part through amending the Articles of Agreement of the International Monetary Fund, comes mainly from powerful Wall Street and Washington interests.[107]

It may be that some countries, influenced by such lines of thought, will follow the already-existing Chilean example in imposing precautionary restrictions on short-term borrowing from abroad, or even, like the government of Malaysia in September 1998, introduce wide-ranging exchange controls. It remains to be seen, however, whether restrictions of the latter kind can be made to work and will yield benefits, real or perceived, which more than offset what are likely to be the substantial costs arising from the complexities and distortions involved and the effects on the confidence of investors both foreign and domestic.

In relation to this current debate, the earlier experience of the OECD countries is relevant. Two morals in particular can be drawn from it.

The first is that country circumstances matter. Generally speaking, and leaving aside the establishment in Europe of the Single Market, the process of freeing external capital flows in the core OECD countries was neither even nor uniform. Countries accepted liberalisation as a goal while choosing for themselves – albeit with provision for mutual consultation and surveillance – the nature and timing of specific measures. In the process, collective ageement on the freeing of short-term capital movements came last: it was only in 1989 that the OECD Codes of Liberalisation were extended to cover all remaining capital flows 'including short-term capital movements, such as money-market transactions, operations

---

[107] Jagdish Bhagwati, 'The Capital Myth: The Difference between Trade in Widgets and Dollars', *Foreign Affairs*, Vol. 77, No. 3, May-June 1998. The quotations are from pp. 8 and 11.

in forward markets, swaps, options, and other derivative instruments'.[108] When applications for OECD membership were made in the 1990s, adherence to the Codes of Liberalisation, together with an agreed negotiated timetable for further freeing of capital flows, was a condition of accession; and all the five countries concerned have carried liberalisation further since they applied for accession, with the eventual abolition of exchange controls as one of the agreed objectives. But as with other members, the choice and timing of changes is for each national government to decide, and in four of these five newcomers, the exception being Mexico, the controls on capital flows that remain are, generally speaking and for the time being, more restrictive than in the core countries.

This OECD experience suggests that the strength of the case for freeing short-term capital movements, and decisions as to how and when to move in this direction, depends on each country's situation. This is in fact the approach adopted by (among others) the IMF, which so far from advocating total and immediate lifting of restrictions has taken the line that 'there are important preconditions for an orderly liberalization of capital movements'.[109]

OECD experience in the last few years further suggests – though this is more debatable – that once the 'preconditions' have been broadly met and controls have been removed, the change should be treated as permanent. This view seems indeed to be widely though not always explicitly held, for it is noteworthy that few commentators, even among those most distrustful of international capital flows, have argued that, in the light of the East Asian developments, the core OECD countries should now reverse course and bring back their former controls. So far at least, none of the governments concerned has considered this step; and even for the five newer members, including Korea, it is not at present under serious consideration. This suggests that the general case for closer restriction – as distinct from arguments that may apply, and then perhaps only temporarily, to particular non-OECD countries – has

---

[108] Pierre Poret, 'Capital Market Liberalisation: OECD Approach and Rules', paper presented to an IMF seminar, 1998. The paper gives a good summary account of the whole history.

[109] *World Economic Outlook*, May 1998, p. 7.

not been made out.

The Case of Korea

Aside from this particular issue, and more fundamentally, these recent crises have in fact reinforced the case for extending economic reform in East Asia, and indeed elsewhere. Korea provides a good illustration. Admittedly, there is little doubt that in the Korean crisis foreign short-term capital flows, as in many other episodes past and current, were destabilising; but the reasons why they had such devastating effects are partly to be found within the Korean economy itself: as with the other East Asian countries affected, a pure 'externalist' explanation of the crisis is not adequate.

In this connection, the OECD Secretariat has made the point that in Korea there was 'financial vulnerability stemming from highly-leveraged firms and a weak, poorly supervised financial system'.[110] To this it can be added

- that many of the highly-leveraged firms had over-invested;
- that the extent of both the over-investment and their over-exposure to debt can be partly accounted for by their being specially favoured by government;
- that much of the debt financing was channelled through banks, some of which were government-owned, all of which were subject to official direction, and many of which were already carrying non-performing loans;
- that the liberalisation of capital inflows which preceded the crisis was limited to 'short-term inflows unnecessarily channelled through banks';[111]
- that close connections between government, banks and favoured firms encouraged the idea that institutions which got into trouble would be rescued; and
- that it was difficult or impossible to check from up-to-date published figures the financial viability of these institutions.

These weaknesses have been recognised, with the result that the response to the crisis in Korea has partly taken the form of a range

---

[110] OECD, *Economic Outlook 63*, preliminary edition, April 1998, p. 205.

[111] OECD, *Economic Outlook 63*, Paris, 1998, p. 12.

of liberalising measures. To quote the OECD Secretariat once more:

> 'The government has taken a number of steps intended to open capital markets, restructure the financial system and strengthen prudential supervision, increase labour market flexibility and encourage corporate restructuring. Additional steps to improve corporate governance practices and further open the product market are planned.'[112]

Broadly similar measures are being taken by governments in the other East Asian countries affected, aside from Malaysia, either independently or in the context of agreements with the international lending institutions. In all these cases, and even if some new forms of restriction on short-term capital movements are imposed, whether temporarily or for a longer period, the result is likely to be a permanent move away from some long-accepted forms of interventionism. It is not only in East Asia that such tendencies may appear.[113]

Hence one effect of the East Asian crises and some related episodes may well be to reinforce on balance the already existing momentum of reform. However, it would be wrong to draw the conclusion, from this and the previous section of the argument, that interventionism has entered into a terminal and irreversible decline. Both domestically and on the international scene there are influences and tendencies which may set limits to further liberalisation, or give rise to a revival of interventionism in forms both old and new.

Old Limits and New Threats

As to domestic policies, reforms so far have chiefly affected the production of marketed goods and services. In the core OECD countries and others, the scope of markets has been extended, and their working improved, in areas where market mechanisms, while subject to numerous and diverse forms of often heavy-handed intervention, were already well established and taken for granted by

---

[112] OECD, *Economic Outlook 63*, p. 104.

[113] Much the same diagnosis and conclusions as here are to be found in Pierre Poret, 'The Case for Orderly Liberalisation in Emerging Market Economies', *OECD Observer*, No. 214, September-October 1998.

virtually everyone. In the former communist countries also, the main reforms have been in these same areas. It is here that liberalisation has gone furthest across the world, through measures that are unlikely to be reversed and which may well spread to countries that have not yet adopted them.

Beyond this, the prospects for further and continuing economic reform are more doubtful. On present indications, this is true in particular of three broad areas of policy where the case for greater economic freedom is still not widely accepted: the provision of free or heavily subsidised public services, including health and education; fiscal transfers, including state pensions and benefits of various kinds; and labour markets. Although in a growing number of countries these areas have been subject to reforming initiatives, there remains a wide gulf between the ideas of economic liberalism and current thinking and practice.

Two brief illustrations will serve to make the point. In education, the argument was made by John Stuart Mill a century and a half ago that government financing need not, and probably should not, imply government provision of the services thus paid for. In 1875 much the same case was put by Karl Marx, who then wrote:

> '"*Elementary education by the state*" is altogether objectionable. Defining by a general law the financial means of the elementary schools, the qualifications of the teachers, the branches of instruction, etc., and... supervising the fulfilment of these legal specifications by state inspectors, is a very different thing from appointing the state as the educator of the people! Government and church should rather be equally excluded from any influence on the school.'

Marx goes on to assert that 'the whole programme... is tainted through and through by the Lassallean sect's servile belief in the state...'[114]

From a liberal viewpoint, this approach is equally relevant today. In the provision of education services, as elsewhere in the economy, there is good reason to believe that consumers should be

---

[114] Karl Marx, *Critique of the Gotha Programme*, written in 1875 though first published only in 1891. The text quoted here is from p. 42 of an edition published in Moscow in 1947 by the Foreign Languages Publishing House. The italics are in the original – Marx was quoting from the text of the Programme.

free to choose between alternatives, that individuals and businesses should be free to enter the industry and to advertise and supply services, and that competition between suppliers would not only widen the range of choice but also make for greater efficiency of operation, regard for consumers and readiness to innovate. Almost everywhere, however, the provision of free schooling remains largely or wholly a public monopoly, nor – though local experiments with greater freedom are to be found, perhaps increasingly – is there any country in which this situation seems about to change.

In labour markets too, prevailing systems and practices, and the received ideas which lend support to them, remain far removed from liberal norms – in some respects, as it appears, increasingly so. There is of course room for debate as to just how these norms should be defined and interpreted. But from a liberal standpoint it is natural to take freedom of contract as a general principle, a point of departure. This implies a presumption against statutory restrictions or legal constraints, both on the freedom of employers and employees to make whatever deals may suit them, with or without the participation of unions, and on wages or conditions of employment including hours worked, paid holidays and age of retirement. It is likewise inconsistent with general legal restrictions deriving from the notion of unfair dismissal, and with anti-discrimination or 'affirmative action' clauses, or quotas whether formal or informal, that limit the range of possible bargains and arrangements for mutual benefit. As Milton Friedman noted in *Capitalism and Freedom* nearly four decades ago:

> '"Fair employment practice" legislation, which aims to prevent discrimination by reasons of race, color or religion [and he would now have to add, by sex, age, national or social origin, political opinions, marital status, sexual preference, or absence of disability] interferes with the freedom of individuals to enter into voluntary contracts with one another.'[115]

At present, a non-restrictive legal framework giving expression to he principle of freedom of contract is not to be found in any country – Hong Kong probably comes closest to it – and there seem

---

[115] Milton Friedman, *Capitalism and Freedom*, Chicago: University of Chicago Press, 1962, p. 115.

to be few cases in which the prevailing trend in labour markets, even in these recent years of economic reform, has clearly and consistently been in that direction. Even in New Zealand after the Employment Contracts Act of 1991, there remain unfair dismissal laws administered by a specialist Employment Court, a statutory minimum wage and other legal provisions governing conditions of work, and anti-discrimination laws which as in other countries significantly restrict the freedom to hire and fire, and which have increased over time in scope and intrusiveness. Nowhere is it widely accepted by public opinion that labour markets should be made substantially freer.

As to the international dimension, traditional protectionism is, as ever, flourishing all over the world, even though it has been losing rather than gaining ground in recent years. Future advances towards freer trade are therefore likely to continue to be hard won. Moreover, it is possible, indeed probable, that the process of international economic integration will be obstructed or partly reversed by new forms of interventionism. In particular, cross-border trade flows may well become increasingly subject to provisions, whether internationally agreed on or unilaterally imposed by the richer countries, relating to minimum international labour standards and environmental regulations; and it is likely that many of these, in so far as they are made effective, will have disintegrating consequences for the world economy. It is often argued, not without cause, that the imposition of such international norms and standards is advocated for protectionist reasons, by employers and unions in the richer countries. But this is not the main point. Even if the motives that lay behind them were entirely disinterested, *such measures would still be open to objection* in so far as they restrict the freedom to enter into non-coercive bargains for mutual gain. Protectionist or not, they are liable to be forces for disintegration.[116]

New restrictive norms are not the only sources of risk to the open multilateral trading and investment system. It could well be

---

[116] Here again, Marx's views are worth recording. At the end of the *Critique of the Gotha Programme,* he condemned not only the general prohibition of child labour, but also – and in this case, with anger and contempt, any denial of opportunity for prisoners to undertake productive labour.

undermined also (1) by a spread of, and greater resort to, anti-dumping actions, and (2) by a growing propensity on the part of one or both of the two largest trading entities, the EU and the US, to adopt unilateral coercive measures, sometimes in the name of market opening. Thus, despite the Uruguay Round agreements and the Bogor Declaration,[117] and the continuing momentum of decontrol in many developing and former communist countries, the further progress of cross-border liberalisation of trade and investment is far from being assured. At the same time, it seems probable that the possibilities for international migration will remain closely restricted, often for reasons, and in ways, that are inconsistent with liberal thinking.

Hence it is not at all certain that interventionism will continue on balance to lose ground over the medium and longer term: the reasonably predictable further gains for liberalism may prove to be both restricted in scope and subject to erosion of various kinds. On the other side of the account, however, there are factors which are already lending support to the liberal trend, and which may well gain in strength.

A Continuing Impetus to Liberalisation

Under this heading, two widely felt influences making for reform can be identified, though their full effects are yet to be seen and are uncertain. The *first* is internal. For most of the present OECD countries, and probably for others too, pressures are likely to arise, or to grow more intense, from what has been called the fiscal crisis of the modern state. Many governments will have little choice but to rethink their systems of public transfers and free or subsidised provision of services, if only because of the further ageing of their populations and the reluctance of voters to accept still higher levels of taxation. By the same token, they will be looking, even more searchingly than now, for ways in which public expenditure programmes generally can be trimmed, run more efficiently,

---

[117] The Bogor Declaration of 1994 was signed by the member countries of the Asia Pacific Economic Cooperation agreement, which include the US and Japan. It commits each of the signatories to establish 'free and open trade and investment' by a specified date – 2010 in the case of the richer members, and 2020 for those that are classed as developing countries. Not surprisingly, there have since been signs that the notion of 'free' trade is subject to varying interpretations by signatories.

financed through charging, or run by private operators. This will influence the direction and content of future reform programmes; and it could well happen, as in the case of privatisation, that ideas for reform which were previously viewed as visionary, impracticable or hopelessly unpopular will progressively win acceptance – in some cases, after they have actually been introduced by harassed or determined governments. There is a case for far-reaching market-oriented reforms in relation to many areas of policy which have not so far been greatly affected by liberalisation: in education, health, social welfare programmes, pensions, housing, town planning and land use, and transport including especially the use of roads, there is a wide range of possibilities – in particular, through introducing or raising fees and charges, extending the scope for competition and private initiative, and making possible or establishing better pricing systems. Hence an extensive though difficult reform agenda is to be found here, which may increasingly enter into practical politics. Once such a tendency has emerged in a few countries, it may gather strength across the world in much the same way as privatisation has done.

A *second* factor, which is international rather than domestic, is the constraining effect of closer cross-border economic integration: the impact of 'globalisation', which up to now has been less marked than is often suggested, may become increasingly felt. For example, it is likely that continuing pressures for tax reform will arise from a wish not to get too far out of line with the practice of other countries where rates have been brought down, and that governments will continue to accede to deregulation in order to help business enterprises within their borders to remain competitive in world markets. More broadly, national governments are becoming increasingly aware of the need to maintain policy régimes which internationally-minded and potentially mobile enterprises will find acceptable. At the same time, further developments in communications, and in particular the growth in transactions carried out via the Internet, may make it harder to enforce official restrictions on the ability of people and businesses to pursue their interests and make unregulated deals.[118]

---

[118] As noted above, an analysis on these lines is developed in Richard B. McKenzie and Dwight R. Lee, *Quicksilver Capital: How the Rapid Movement of Wealth Has Changed*

It is possible that in response to these and other developments, the liberal semi-consensus will gain further strength, and governments will continue to take the path of reform – not solely, or even typically, from a belief in economic liberalism as such, but rather as a means to dealing with problem situations, or simply because they have lost the ability to enforce particular regulations which limit people's choices. Hence there may well be a continuing impetus to liberalisation, not only in ways that have now become well established and broadly accepted by public opinion, but also in areas of policy where so far there has been much less to show. Social changes, which in part arise from liberalisation itself, may contribute to its extension on these lines. Rising average real incomes, wider share ownership, the growth of self-employment and contracting for labour services, the decline of trade unionism in the private sector, and the shrinking of the public sector where unionism and anti-competitive attitudes remain dominant, are likely to be influences on the side of reform.[119]

Rather than trying to turn this brief review of possibilities into predictions or a set of scenarios, I conclude by setting the events of these last two decades in a much longer historical perspective. In doing so, I draw together some of the main threads from the argument so far, while joining them up with one or two new ones.

---

the World, New York: The Free Press, 1991. They argue (p. xi) that as a result of the growth of cross-border capital mobility and closer integration of national economies, 'governments have lost much of the monopoly power that undergirded their growth in earlier decades' – a process that is still under way.

[119] Arthur Seldon, in a recently-published study, has argued that in present-day democracies government 'has lost the power to maintain its economic empire', because increasingly people are able to escape from the sphere of public tax-financed provision. The means of escape are provided by new products and methods, higher incomes, the growing scope for work outside employment contracts, the 'parallel' or 'grey' economy, possibilities of barter, the development of electronic means of payment, the growth of transactions via the Internet, and the process of closer international economic integration. (Arthur Seldon, *The Dilemma of Democracy: The Political Economics of Over-Government*, Hobart Paper No. 136, London: Institute of Economic Affairs, 1998.)

Part 5: Epilogue: A 120-Year Perspective

FRANCIS FUKUYAMA HAS ARGUED THAT 'the worldwide liberal revolution' which he sees as being now in progress represents the prolongation of a centuries-old tendency which can be expected to continue. He writes:

> '...the growth of liberal democracy, together with its companion, economic liberalism, has been the most remarkable macropolitical phenomenon of the last four hundred years... the current liberal revolution...constitutes further evidence that there is a fundamental process at work that dictates a common evolutionary pattern for *all* human societies – in short, something like a Universal History of mankind in the direction of liberal democracy. The existence of peaks and troughs in this development is undeniable. But...Cycles and discontinuities in themselves are not incompatible with a history that is directional and universal...'.[120]

This view of the past may be valid for liberal democracy, but does not at all apply to its 'companion'. For one thing, the time-frame of 400 years does not fit. On the one hand, the story of economic freedom goes a long way back, much further than four centuries. Thus Hayek maintains, in relation to the history of Rome, that 'The classical period was ...a period of complete economic freedom, to which Rome largely owed its prosperity and peace', while Sir John Hicks traced the origins of what he termed the Mercantile Economy to the emergence of the city state as a trading entity.[121] On the other hand, economic liberalism as a doctrine, a coherent way of thinking about economic and political systems with a broad programme to go with it, goes back only some two centuries and a half. To quote Lionel Robbins:

> 'Only in the middle of the eighteenth century did men begin to conceive of a world in which privilege to restrict should itself be restricted and in which the disposition of resources should obey, not the demands of producers for monopoly, but the demands of consumers for wealth.'[122]

---

[120] Francis Fukuyama, *The End of History and the Last Man*, New York: Avon Books, 1993, p. 48.

[121] Hayek, *The Constitution of Liberty, op. cit.*, p. 107; John Hicks, *A Theory of Economic History*, Oxford: Clarendon Press, 1969.

[122] Lionel Robbins, *Economic Planning and International Order*, London: Macmillan,

A Century-Long Retreat

Over this 250 years as a whole, contrary to Fukuyama's thesis, there has been no consistent trend to economic liberalism. True, there was clearly such a tendency, over a growing number of countries, from the latter part of the 18th century onwards; but from the late 19th century this direction of change was reversed. Liberalism began on balance to lose ground, and was increasingly and explicitly rejected. Although there is no conspicuous and dramatic turning point, 1880 can be taken as an approximate watershed year; and as was seen in Part 1 above, the recent trend away from interventionism in economic systems can be dated, again approximately, from the close of the 1970s. Over the whole of the intervening century, on balance, economic systems, and in some respects economic ideas also, moved away from liberal norms and practice. This was not a matter of 'cycles and discontinuities', to use Fukuyama's terms. Before the present trend set in, and even allowing for exceptions and for some notable positive developments after 1945, *economic liberalism had been in decline for a century*. This makes recent events the more remarkable; and in looking ahead, it is worth examining the main features of past decline and present recovery, with a view to distinguishing those recent changes that may be temporary or reversible from those that appear more permanent and likely to be taken further.

In viewing the past 120 years, the two world wars emerge as landmark events. Hence there are three main phases to consider: 1880-1914; 1914-45; and the period since the Second World War. Within the latter, the last 20 years form a distinct sub-period in which a long-continuing downward trend in the fortunes of economic liberalism has been reversed.

The main aspects and features of liberal decline after 1880 are all to be seen before the First World War. Three in particular are to be noted, both because they involved a clear break with liberalism and because they were woven together to make up a rival and increasingly influential view of the world.

The *first* of these comprises policies towards international trade. During the decades before the First World War, an increasing

1937, p. 233.

number of countries in Europe, together with Canada and later followed by Australia, New Zealand and Japan, moved to establish protective tariffs – thus joining the US and Russia, which had never adopted free trade. By later standards, almost all the protective systems of mid-1914 were moderate; and on balance, and despite them, closer international economic integration went ahead during this whole period. All the same, free trade had been generally discarded as a guiding principle.

The *second* area is that of foreign and colonial policies. Not surprisingly, governments across the world had never been strongly influenced by Cobdenite liberal ways of viewing national interests and international relations, except – for a period only, from roughly 1860 to 1880 – in the context of treaties providing for free trade; and from the 1890s, as David Fieldhouse has noted, imperialism acquired a more purposive and systematic character: 'European statesmen and public opinion began to assume that each state must stake its claims overseas or see national interests go by default.'[123] In some cases, as in French practice and in the programme put forward in Britain by Joseph Chamberlain, such notions were linked to preferential tariff systems and ideas of imperial strategic self-reliance in a world of great-power rivalries. Tariff protection and imperial preferences were viewed not just as instruments for shielding and encouraging particular industries or ventures, but also as leading elements in national self-assertion and defence.

The *third* main element is domestic. Over this same period, national governments increasingly assumed responsibility for (1) redistributing income and wealth through public finance, (2) the establishment of nation-wide schemes for pensions and social insurance of various kinds, (3) the financing, and increasingly the provision, of education and health services, and in many cases (4) the closer regulation of labour markets. How far the underlying aims of these often related initiatives represented a break with economic liberalism, rather than a legitimate reinterpretation and reshaping of it to meet changing conditions and new possibilities, is to some extent debatable: as noted above, there are – and were – different schools of thought within the liberal camp, particularly

---

[123] David Fieldhouse, *Economics and Empire*, London: Weidenfeld and Nicolson, 1973, p. 463.

with respect to redistribution through public finance. But the extent of centralisation and state provision in the various expenditure programmes, and the limits thus placed on competition and freedom of choice and initiative, typically went much further than was consistent with the principle of limited government. As Hayek noted in relation to Bismarck's initiative in Germany in the 1880s, which created the first centrally-sponsored social insurance system:

> '…individuals were not merely required to make provision against those risks which, if they did not, the state would have to provide for, but were compelled to obtain this protection through a unitary organization run by the government… Social insurance…from the beginning meant not merely compulsory insurance but compulsory membership in a unitary organization controlled by the state.'[124]

Almost everywhere, centralisation within such schemes, as also in health and education, brought with it an undermining of the existing voluntary organisations and charities, a narrowing of options, and the creation of whole new categories of people who were servants of the state.

Thus even by 1914 the notion had become widely accepted, not just among socialists, that economic liberalism was an outdated creed. Official policies naturally reflected this, and these policies were not made by socialist parties which up to then had nowhere won office. It was in fact the conservative nationalist framework of thinking, and governments that reflected it, which provided an increasingly accepted alternative to liberalism, particularly in the imperial Germany of 1871-1918 whose influence on world events proved decisive. This alternative combined collectivist social policies, tariff protection, and a conception of national interest as being served by military power, assertiveness, and the possession or control of trade routes and territory. Its influence and appeal were not confined to parties and movements of the right.

The First World War itself, and still more its consequences, brought a whole series of setbacks to the liberal cause. As an immediate result, a fully state-directed economic system emerged in what was to become the USSR, while everywhere the wartime experience of government direction increased the tendency to

---

[124] Hayek, *The Constitution of Liberty, op. cit.*, p. 287.

accept regulation as normal, and reinforced the sense and conviction that the natural trend of events was towards a larger economic role for the state. Even in the 1920s, tariff rates were typically increased, while new tariff systems came into existence as a result of the emergence of newly-created national states. Then, with the advent and deepening of the Great Depression, the international trade and payments system was shattered. Virtually every country raised tariffs, while alongside them import quotas became a standard instrument of policy. Exchange controls were widely adopted and international flows of long-term investment fell away. Between 1929 and 1932 the volume of world exports declined by more than one-quarter, while in value terms the fall was over 60 per cent.[125] Everywhere the relatively free movement of people across national borders, which had been largely preserved up to 1914, was replaced by highly restrictive immigration régimes. The whole notion of a predominantly *laissez-faire* capitalist economy was discredited by the onset and persistence of mass unemployment, the more so since no such trend had appeared in the Soviet Union. Just as later in the 1970s, governments everywhere reacted to unforeseen problems and crises with a range of interventionist measures, domestic and external. Under the impact of events, economic thinking moved towards a more activist conception of the role of governments. By the end of the inter-war period it was widely accepted that liberalism was finished, driven from the stage by the march of events. A good illustration is the valedictory judgement made by an eminent (and liberal) economic historian, Eli Heckscher, writing in the early 1930s, that:

> 'mercantilism gave way to liberalism which, after a period of dominance which represented a very short time in world history, gave way in its turn to newer systems.'[126]

Into this scene, as a further and calamitous element of disintegration, came the Nazi régime in Germany, and with it the harnessing of what soon became the strongest military power in the world to Hitler's conception of a national destiny to be realised through war, conquest, the confiscation of vast territories, and the

---

[125] These estimates are from Maddison, *Monitoring the World Economy, op. cit.*, pp. 238-39.

[126] Heckscher, *Mercantilism, op. cit.*, Vol. 2, p. 339.

establishment of a master race. This belongs in our story, not just because it made a second European war virtually inevitable, but because it represented an extension and fulfilment, carried it is true to the point of utter insanity, of the related notions which had so gained ground even before 1914 – the submergence of individual goals into those of the nation, the collectivist view of the state's role, responsibilities and powers to act, and the idea of conquest as the key to realising not only national security and prosperity but also, and more fundamentally, the task assigned by history to the nation and those belonging to it.

In a less extreme and irrational form, much the same notions underlay the evolution of Japanese imperial and foreign policy in the decade or so before Pearl Harbour. The plan which took shape for a 'Co-Prosperity Sphere' has obvious affinities with earlier notions, in Britain and Germany especially, of imperial self-sufficiency and the control of strategic overseas territories as a necessary basis for a country's security and influence in the world, and hence (it was assumed) for prosperity also. It is not just military-dominated *Realpolitik* that accounts for Japanese official policies in these years, but also a more widely held conception of national interests, and of the means to pursuing them, which was profoundly collectivist and anti-liberal, and where the possibility of sustained economic progress within a free and open economy was not so much rejected as scarcely recognised. There are few starker and more fateful instances in history of the continuing influence on political leaders of pre-economic conceptions of the world.

As a result of the Second World War, the immediate frontal attack on liberalism, political and economic, was repelled, and before long fully-functioning democratic systems and relatively free market economies were established in both Germany and Japan – indeed, the German economic reforms of the late 1940s were a landmark event in the history of economic liberalism. At the same time, this war, like its predecessor, contributed both to extending central control over the economy and to reinforcing the idea that this was still the natural trend of events. Further, an early momentous consequence of the war was the establishment of communism and state-directed economies in Central and Eastern Europe, while before long the same had happened in China and North Vietnam. For the non-communist world, the summary

116

history from the early post-war years to the late 1970s is set out in Part 1 above: briefly, it records (1) a mixed story for the core OECD countries, with liberalism gaining ground on balance from 1945 to 1973, but with some retreat over the next few years, and (2) for the developing countries as a group, though with exceptions, a general trend towards interventionism. For the world as a whole over this period, and taking account of all three groups of countries, it is the counter-liberal tendencies that on balance prevail.

Has the Climate of Opinion Really Changed?

This survey of history might suggest a darker view of the prospects for economic liberalism than was initially sketched above, since within it these last two decades emerge as a relatively short and possibly unrepresentative phase, following a century-long broadly unfavourable trend. To judge this, it is helpful to look at the three main heads of anti-liberal thinking and practice just identified – protectionism, nationalism and collectivism – and to see how far, in relation to each, the liberal alternative has made gains which could well be lasting. Here much depends on an assessment of how far underlying attitudes have changed and are changing.

In relation to this movement of attitudes, there is some difference between the external and internal dimensions of policy. With respect to international transactions, including capital flows as well as trade, there has been continuing and extensive liberalisation in a process which has spread in recent years from the core OECD countries to much of the rest of the world. For the OECD group this trend, despite the many limitations, qualifications and exceptions that have attended it, goes back half a century to the resolutions and agreements of the early post-war years: it is not just a recent change of course. For the non-OECD countries involved, old assumptions have been set aside in response to what have appeared as the lessons of past decades, and this may well prove to be a lasting change. In both groups, and even taking into account the impact of the recent financial crises, there is an established momentum of liberalisation which, in part because of the continuing effects of the revolution in communications, seems likely to be maintained. True, there is another side to the picture. Trade interventionism in a variety of forms is to be found still in pretty well every country and trading entity; the ideas of traditional mercantilism remain widely

117

influential; there is considerable distrust, especially though not only in many developing countries, of the idea of closer international economic integration; and there exists now a substantial risk that trade will be distorted by damaging new provisions relating to employment conditions and environmental standards. Further, and as noted above, the idea of full freedom of capital flows has now become more widely questioned, at any rate for non-OECD economies. All the same, *a relatively open and non-interventionist world trade and investment system has almost certainly come to stay.* Indeed, it is now possible to imagine, for the first time since June 1914, the re-establishment of a liberal international economic order extending to all cross-border flows except those of people.

The change in attitudes here has gone together with a profound – though incomplete and not fully explicit – recasting of the assumptions underlying foreign policies and the conduct of international relations. Three main factors have been at work here. *First* is the restoration and spread of liberal democratic régimes and institutions. This has restricted the possibilities for assertive nationalism, since there is good reason to think that 'modern democracies do not go to war with one another', and that 'The slow growth of stable democracy will gradually extend the area in which nations do not need to fear being conquered or destroyed'.[127] The transformation of the relationship between France and Germany since 1945 is a conspicuous instance of how the world has changed in this respect. *Second,* the growth and spread of prosperity since the Second World War has made it evident as never before that the key to a better material life is not to be found in the acquisition and control of foreign or colonial territory: in this, Cobden has at last begun to come into his own. *Third,* the collapse of communism has meant that for the first time since the revolution of 1917 the foreign policy of Russia is not based on the unwavering assumption of permanent hostility towards, and on the part of, the Western capitalist countries. All this has not only strengthened the prospects for peace, which itself is favourable to economic liberalism; it has also further undermined the ideas and assumptions of collectivist

---

[127] Max Singer and Aaron Wildavsky, *The Real World Order: Zones of Peace/ Zones of Turmoil*, Chatham, NJ: Chatham House Publishers Inc., 1993, pp. 3 and 4.

nationalism and *raison d'état*, and thus done much to remove from the scene what had always been a powerful anti-liberal influence.

When it comes to domestic policies, the record of change looks rather different and the prospects more uncertain. On the one hand, there are a number of respects in which underlying attitudes and assumptions have changed significantly and the change could well prove lasting. Across the world, this can be seen in the acceptance and spread of privatisation and 'marketisation' – through the transfer of ownership from public to private hands, the contracting out of the provision of public services, and (though this remains more difficult) the raising or introduction of charges for these. In the core OECD countries, the widespread resistance to higher taxes, and concern about their effects, has meant that attempts to limit public expenditure are now an established feature of government policies. Elsewhere in the world, among the sizeable minority of non-reforming countries, there is a good chance that the further spread of democracy will lead to the establishment or restoration of basic economic freedoms, as well as to greater openness to trade and investment, in the countries affected. In every country, the combined effect of modern communications and the cross-border liberalisation that has already occurred has been to make people aware as never before of wider economic possibilities and opportunities, and hence more resistant to forms of regulation, internal as well as external, which would close them off. This tendency can be expected to continue.

Perhaps more than on the external side, however, there are qualifications to be made to this story of economic reforms and of support for liberalisation. In the core OECD countries in particular, public expenditure ratios for the most part remain at high and close to record levels. In almost every country, labour markets are still closely regulated; free schooling, most social services, and often the supply of health services continue to be dominated by state monopoly provision; and the permeation of economic life by political influences is even now largely accepted or endorsed. All this reflects a strong continuity of anti-liberal ideas, assumptions and attitudes, as well as – and arguably more than – the combination of successful lobbying by interest groups and self-directed preoccupations on the part of political leaders. In most if not all countries, including those which have recently emerged from communist systems, there remains a surprising degree of belief in the capacity and duty of central governments to manage national economies in detail, and to bring to pass a wide range of specific outcomes without noticeable cost to individual freedom or the effective working of the system. The obverse of this attitude, as noted already, is a general distrust of markets and non-regulated processes. In relation to the recent and prospective success of liberal democracy, Fukuyama argues convincingly that authoritarian régimes have lost legitimacy in the world of today: almost everywhere, their claims to acceptance and support are now dismissed as fraudulent. *Broadly speaking, and despite the collapse of communism, no such decisive loss of perceived legitimacy has yet occurred with respect to the economic role and pretensions of the modern state.*

An Achievement and Its Limits

When viewed in the perspective of the last 120 years, the recent clear improvement in the fortunes of economic liberalism appears as more impressive and more fundamental, and yet at the same time more surprising. The fact that a century-long decline has been so clearly reversed, with a large and growing majority of countries around the world taking the path of economic reform, is remarkable in itself; and in the light of history, it is apparent that the significance of what has happened goes well beyond a listing of specific reforms and changes of course in policies. There have been profound shifts in attitudes and working assumptions. From the late 19th century for many decades, national economic policies, internal and external, were strongly influenced, if not dominated, by the two leading and mutually reinforcing constituents of anti-liberal thinking and practice – that is, economic nationalism, joined with a belief in the need for central direction of economic systems, or at any rate for a continuing expansion of state ownership and state initiative. Both of these twin guiding principles have lost authority and support: it is they, rather than the liberal view of the world, which now increasingly appear as outdated and inadequate. Few predicted before the event that the climate of opinion would evolve in this way.

It would be wrong, however, to conclude from this change, and from the recent progress of economic reform, that liberalism as such has triumphed or is in course of doing so, still less that such an outcome is historically natural or inevitable. As we have seen, the liberalisation of these past two decades, and the change in attitudes which it has both reflected and helped to promote, have not been mainly due to, and have not brought about, a general endorsement of economic liberalism as such. Today as earlier, the ideas which enter into the liberal blueprint, despite the gains they have made within the extended professional milieu, have only limited support elsewhere: it is a telling fact that they do not even now provide the basis, in any country of the world, for a political movement or party that has to be taken seriously in the competition for office and power. In effect, public opinion and political leaders across the world have come to accept some of the leading practical conclusions that liberalism points to, while remaining indifferent to, or distrustful of, the way of thinking from which these conclusions are derived.

There is little sign that this situation is about to change. On the positive side (from a liberal viewpoint), a general reversal of the main recent market-oriented reforms does not now seem probable in any leading country, while there are reasons for thinking that the pressures and incentives arising both from events and problem situations and from further technical progress will continue on balance to favour the liberal cause, as they have over the past two decades. At the same time, however, the various anti-liberal influences described above are likely everywhere to remain both strong and pervasive, and it is possible that in many countries they will gain at least temporary strength from untoward developments, economic and political, which cannot now be clearly foreseen, or from reactions to what are seen as the adverse consequences of liberalisation and closer international economic integration. Even aside from such possibilities of retreat, the further extension of market-oriented reforms to those areas of policy which have so far remained relatively unaffected by liberalisation is very much in question. Despite their substantial improvement over these past two decades, which appears all the more notable when seen in historical perspective, the fortunes of economic liberalism during the opening decades of the new century remain clouded and in doubt.

ANNEX

Measuring Economic Freedom and Assessing Its Benefits[1]

The Economic Freedom of the World Project, some of the recent results of which are drawn on in Chapter II above, has been sponsored by a network of research institutes across the world, including the Institute of Economic Affairs, under the leadership of the Fraser Institute of Vancouver, Canada. The main research has been carried out at Florida State University, under the direction of James Gwartney. From its early days, Milton Friedman has been a sponsor of, and adviser to, the project. The main output is the set of economic freedom ratings for a growing number of countries across the world over the period from 1975 onwards, but the results are also used to explore the relationship between the extent of freedom and both the level of GDP per head and its rate of growth in the countries covered: an underlying theme, therefore, is the relation between economic freedom and economic performance.

Derivation of the Index of Economic Freedom

The ratings for each country are arrived at by judging its performance under a set of 17 attributes which, when combined, make up an index of economic freedom: each attribute is assigned a weight, and each country's overall freedom rating is the weighted average of its 17 individual ratings. The attributes are grouped under four headings, namely:

- 'Money and inflation' (total weight, 15.7 out of 100), which covers the rate of growth of the money supply, recent inflation rates, and the freedom of citizens to hold foreign currency and to bank abroad.

- 'Government operations and regulations' (total weight, 34.6), which covers the share of government consumption in total consumption, the significance of public enterprises, the extent

---

[1] This Annex draws on a review article of mine on the first main report of the Economic Freedom of the World Project, *Economic Freedom of the World, 1975-95*. (David Henderson, 'Measuring Economic Freedom and Assessing Its Benefits', *Agenda*, Vol. 4, No. 2, 1997.)

of price controls, freedom of businesses to compete, legal equality and access to a 'non-discriminatory judiciary', and freedom from regulations that cause real interest rates to be negative.

- 'Takings and discriminatory taxation' (total weight, 27.2), which covers transfers and subsidies in relation to GDP, top marginal tax rates and their thresholds, and whether or not there is military conscription.

- 'Restraints on international exchange' (total weight, 22.5), which covers the level of taxes on international trade, the difference between the official and the black market exchange rates, the actual size of the trade sector as compared with what might be expected, and the extent of official restrictions on overseas capital transfers.

In arriving at the rating for a particular country in a particular year, there are unavoidably problems as to (1) the reliability of the published data relating to each of the listed attributes, (2) the mapping of the data into ratings on the scale of zero to 10, as well as (3) the choice of weights for each attribute and the ratings attached to it. So far as I can judge, the project has made a good selection and use of relevant sources, while the choice of procedures under (2) and (3) has been thoroughly considered. Hence the results, in terms of the ratings and their changes over time, are of considerable interest. At the same time, there are limitations not only to the figures themselves, but also to even the most soundly based and best conducted statistical exercise of this kind. Further, and inevitably, there is room for debate as to the significance of what comes out of the study.

Limitations of the Results

There are various limitations and weaknesses to be found in the index in its present form. Not surprisingly, one of these relates to coverage, which though broad is still incomplete. In particular, no indicators have as yet been included relating to the changing balance between freedom and regulation in labour markets; work is now under way to make good this omission. A further gap, not easy to fill, relates to economy-wide regulation in such areas as occupational health and safety and the environment. A specific weakness, which arises from the project's exclusive focus on individual countries, is that the present freedom ratings take no account of the existence of the European Union. Hence a country such as Belgium has been given the maximum rating for its liberal trade régime, despite the fact that Belgium's trade régime has long been that of the EU which (to put it mildly) contains significant non-liberal features. More generally, issues of accuracy and interpretation arise concerning the results that are shown for particular countries. In Australia, for instance, the evolution of the freedom ratings bears surprisingly little correspondence with what most observers would regard as the changing balance within official policies: the main advances are assigned to the period of the Fraser government in 1975-80, whereas it was the succeeding Labour government, from the end of 1983 to the beginning of the 1990s, which took the decisive steps towards a less regulated and more open economy. Such doubts and queries as to accuracy, relevance and completeness are to be expected in what are still the early stages of such an ambitious venture in comparative economic history.

More broadly, there are aspects of the evolution of economic policies, and of the changing balance between liberalism and interventionism, which are not fully captured in statistical series or indicators, however well chosen and assembled. Thus turning points may be critical even though their short-term measurable results are limited: among other instances, this is true for the Australian case just mentioned, and it may likewise prove true of India in 1991. In the case of the former Soviet Union, as noted above in the main text, the various indicators that show restricted progress up to now do not reveal, or even hint at, the momentous fact that a new epoch has begun. Further, an exclusive focus on the measurable dimensions of economic freedom risks giving a distorted picture because the political dimension is not taken into account: as Sir Samuel Brittan has rightly said, 'there are subtle links between political repression and the reality of economic freedom itself, difficult to put into any index'.[2] The high ratings given here for a country such as Singapore may not be fully comparable with those for more open political systems.

---

[2] *Financial Times*, 12 June 1997.

The Connection between Economic Freedom and Economic Performance

In the first major report from the project, *Economic Freedom of the World, 1975-95*, a special chapter is devoted to a cross-country comparative analysis of the relation between the freedom ratings and the success of economic systems as shown by levels of GDP per head and rates of change in it over time: both changes within countries and differences across them are taken into account in the analysis. The evidence from the country data for this 20-year period is marshalled so as to bring out three results which appear as firmly established: *first*, countries with higher freedom ratings have higher levels of GDP per head; *second*, the countries with high freedom ratings had higher rates of growth of GDP per head in the period, as compared with those with low ratings where these rates were generally low and often negative; and *third*, increases in the ratings were characteristically followed by increases in the rates of growth of GDP per head.

These conclusions are not surprising, and the broad connection between economic freedom and prosperity emerges even more strikingly if one goes beyond the study, to take into account evidence which extends further than the 20 years or so which it covers. Between 1945 and 1990 something remarkably close to a controlled country-wide experiment took place, which has thrown into clear relief some of the necessary conditions for good economic performance. In two adjacent economies, quite different economic and political systems were established at the end of the Second World War, and maintained thereafter, where previously there had been only one. At the time when the separation occurred, both countries were in much the same difficult, almost desperate, situation. They shared a common language, a common history, and a common culture and social structure, yet by historical accident they now took separate and contrasted paths. For the next 45 years the two economies evolved on different lines, largely in isolation from one another since one of the governments effectively closed off all interactions between them. Their comparative performance was strikingly and consistently divergent, so much so that eventually the less successful system ceased to be viable and merged with the other.

These two contrasted political and economic systems, of course, belonged respectively to West and East Germany. One could scarcely imagine a more conclusive demonstration of the superiority of a largely market-led system over a state-directed one. A similar contrast, equally telling, is to be found in East Asia, as between South and North Korea.

This, however, leaves open the question of whether and to what extent, *within* the set of countries which have market-based economic systems, growth rates of productivity and output per head are closely linked to the prevailing balance between liberalism and interventionism and to changes in this balance. To my mind, it is clear that other influences, understandably not considered in the Economic Freedom of the World project, may have to be taken into account.

One instance of this is the comparative performance of the British and Japanese economies in the decades after the Second World War. Between 1950 and 1973, on Angus Maddison's figures, the average annual growth rate of GDP per head in Britain was 2.4 per cent, as compared with 8.0 per cent in Japan. Admittedly, this huge gap becomes narrower if one takes instead the respective estimated rates of growth of labour productivity, as measured by GDP per hour worked: for Britain this is 3.1 per cent per annum, as compared with 7.7 per cent for Japan. However, the difference is still very large, so large that it cannot mainly be explained in terms of the 'catch-up factor', which enters in because of the low Japanese starting-point in 1950.

Why was the Japanese economic performance in these years so strikingly better than the British? One widely-accepted explanation is that well-devised official industrial policies, originating in and carried through by the famous MITI (Ministry of International Trade and Industry), were the main single factor: Japan is seen as offering a model of a planned market economy and a 'developmental state'. On this view, so far from it being greater economic freedom that made the difference, it was to the contrary judicious central guidance, of a kind which was lacking in Britain but available in Japan, and which entailed a degree of departure from liberal norms. Even if one rejects this interpretation of history, as I would myself,[3] it is hard to see that the main difference

---

[3] Reasons for doubting that the effects of Japanese governments' post-war industrial policies

127

between the two economies is to be found in the prevailing extent of economic freedom or its comparative evolution, with the Japanese system closer to the liberal blueprint. It is true that nationalisation was carried a good deal further in Britain than in Japan after the Second World War, and that the public expenditure ratio was consistently higher. On the other hand, while both began the period as highly protectionist, it was the UK that did more to liberalise its trade as time went on; Japanese agricultural protection was much higher throughout; and foreign direct investment was virtually precluded in Japan while the British investment régime was consistently liberal. Both countries maintained tight exchange control régimes. Comparing the two economies, it is hard to see how the striking contrast in performance could be explained in terms of differences, or divergent changes, in an index of economic freedom: it seems clear that other influences were dominant.

Other historical episodes point to a similar conclusion. For example, the general and surprisingly abrupt falling away of rates of productivity growth in virtually all the core OECD countries, as between the 'golden age' of 1950-73 and the past quarter of a century, cannot readily be explained in terms of a shift towards interventionism, even though elements of this are arguably part of the story. A more specific and more recent comparison is between the economies of New Zealand and Ireland. Since the reform process was set under way in New Zealand in mid-1984, liberalisation has been taken further there than in Ireland, and on most reckonings the New Zealand economy would now show up as the freer of the two: both these conclusions emerge from the respective figures in Table 3 (above, p. 40). But if we compare 1984 with 1997, GDP per head in New Zealand appears as having increased by only some 10 per cent, as compared with over 90 per cent for Ireland.[4] It seems obvious that this remarkable divergence

___

were significant and positive are set out in Ramesh Ponnuru, *The Mystery of Japanese Growth*, London: Centre for Policy Studies, 1994. In any case, British governments, regardless of party allegiance, pursued systematic activist industrial policies of various kinds right through these years and later.

[4] GDP figures are from OECD sources. Admittedly, this may not be the most appropriate comparison: because inward direct foreign investment has been so important in Ireland, and exceptionally low corporation taxes are in place for many of the firms involved, GNP per head, rather than GDP, might well be a better indication of performance. But such an adjustment would still leave a wide gap between the two countries.

between the two countries cannot be chiefly explained with reference to the comparative extent of economic freedom or differences in the recent progress of liberalisation.

It is in fact doubly misleading to present economic freedoms as providing uniquely the master-key to economic progress. For one thing, and as just noted, this may not fit well the facts of particular historical episodes or situations. But in any case, these freedoms are to be valued for their own sake: they are ends as well as means. That there may be other influences as well on economic performance, and hence other means of improving it, does not weaken the case for trying to secure and maintain them.

The qualifications just made do not put in question the broad conclusions of the Economic Freedom of the World studies. The connection between economic freedom and prosperity is real, and these past few decades have indeed provided strong confirmatory evidence of it. What is more, the connection appears as closer and more pervasive if one takes account also of aspects of material well-being which are not reflected in national accounts statistics. For instance, the freeing or extension of retail opening hours, which has gone ahead in many previously regulated core OECD countries, has brought improvements in welfare, possibly substantial, which do not show up in series for GDP per head; and similar gains have been still greater in former communist countries where rationing and queues were pervasive under the old system. Again, the case against anti-discrimination laws is that they preclude a host of mutually beneficial deals and arrangements: as Richard Epstein has put it in the context of New Zealand, 'every single characteristic regarded as irrelevant under the Human Rights Act 1993 may in some settings be absolutely critical for the intelligent deployment of resources'.[5] The benefits from such an improved deployment, which extend to consumers also, would go well beyond what would be picked up in the series for GDP. It is because the gains arising from free choice, free contract and private initiative are varied, pervasive and widely diffused that the link with prosperity is so direct.

---

[5] Richard Epstein, *Human Rights and Anti-discrimination Legislation*, Wellington: New Zealand Business Roundtable, 1996, p. 14.

Corporate Governance:

Accountability in the Marketplace

Elaine Sternberg

1. Businesses and corporations are not the same thing: not all corporations are businesses, and most businesses are not corporations. Whereas 'business' designates a particular objective, 'corporation' designates a particular organisational structure.

2. Corporate governance refers to ways of ensuring that corporate actions, assets and agents are directed at achieving the corporate objectives established by the corporation's shareholders (as set out in the Memorandum of Association or comparable constitutional document).

3. Many criticisms of corporate governance are based on false assumptions about what constitutes ethical conduct by corporations, and confusions about what corporate governance is.

4. Protests against takeovers, 'short-termism', redundancies and high executive remuneration are typically objections to specific corporate outcomes, not criticisms of corporate governance.

5. Many misguided criticisms of the Anglo-Saxon model come from confusing corporate governance with government: it is a mistake to criticise corporations for not achieving public policy objectives, and for not giving their stakeholders the rights and privileges commonly associated with citizenship.

6. Some criticisms of the traditional Anglo-Saxon model of corporate governance are justified. There are serious practical obstacles that prevent shareholders from keeping their corporations and corporate agents properly accountable.

7. Though commonly praised, the German and Japanese systems are considerably less capable of achieving the definitive purpose of corporate governance than the Anglo-Saxon model is. Neither is designed to protect, nor typically used for protecting, property rights.

8. The increasingly popular stakeholder theory is also incapable of providing better corporate governance. Stakeholder theory is incompatible with all substantial objectives and undermines both private property and accountability.

9. Regulation that attempts to improve corporate governance by limiting shareholders' options, and reducing their freedom to control their own companies as they choose, is necessarily counterproductive.

10. The way to respond to flaws in current Anglo-Saxon corporate governance mechanisms is to improve the accountability of corporations to their ultimate owners, preferably by having corporations compete for investment, and institutional investors for funds, in part on the degree of accountability they offer to their beneficial owners.

The Institute of Economic Affairs

2 Lord North Street, Westminster, London SW1P 3LB
Telephone: 0171 799 3745 Facsimile: 0171 799 2137
E-mail: iea@iea.org.uk Internet: http://www.iea.org.uk   ISBN 0-255 36416-4

£12.00

Regulating Utilities: Understanding the Issues

Utility regulation in Britain has now entered a phase in which debate is no longer so much concerned with whether it is preferable to rival systems but with how to shape the 'regulatory contract' in monopoly areas and, in potentially competitive areas, how to ensure rivalry.

The latest version of this annual volume of Readings, published jointly by the Institute and London Business School, contains papers by eminent commentators on utility regulation and comments by the regulators themselves.

Contents

Introduction
M.E. BEESLEY

1. Regulatory Institutions and Regulatory Policy for Economies in Transition
   MARTIN CAVE AND JON STERN, Comments by SIR BRYAN CARSBERG

2. Local Competition in UK Telecommunications
   MARK ARMSTRONG, Comments by M.E. BEESLEY

3. Progress in Gas Competition
   GEORGE YARROW, Comments by EILEEN MARSHALL

4. Regulatory Asset Value and the Cost of Capital
   GEOFFREY WHITTINGTON, Comments by IAN BYATT

5. Pool Reform and Competition in Electricity
   DAVID NEWBERY, Comments by STEPHEN LITTLECHILD,
   Additional Comments by GEOFFREY HORTON

6. When is Discrimination Undue?
   JOHN VICKERS, Comments by JOHN BRIDGEMAN

7. MMC and Decisions on RPI-x
   MARTIN HOWE, Comments by COLIN ROBINSON

8. What Next in UK Railways?
   JOHN WELSBY, Comments by CHRIS BOLT

£17.00

The Institute of Economic Affairs
2 Lord North Street, Westminster, London SW1P 3LB
Telephone: 0171 799 3745 Facsimile: 0171 799 2137
E-mail: iea@iea.org.uk Internet: http://www.iea.org.uk   ISBN 0-255 36418-0